HERE YOU GO AGAIN,
GOD!

True Stories That Will Inspire You
to Pray for Miracles

LEE HANSON

WESTBOW
P R E S S®
A DIVISION OF THOMAS NELSON
& ZONDERVAN

This book is a work of non-fiction. Unless otherwise noted, the author and the publisher
make no explicit guarantees as to the accuracy of the information contained in this book
and in some cases, names of people and places have been altered to protect their privacy.

Scripture taken from the King James Version of the Bible.

Scripture taken from the New King James Version®. Copyright © 1982
by Thomas Nelson. Used by permission. All rights reserved.

Scripture quotations marked (NIV) are taken from the Holy Bible, New
International Version®, NIV®. Copyright © 1973, 1978, 1984, 2011 by Biblica,
Inc.™ Used by permission of Zondervan. All rights reserved worldwide. www.
zondervan.com The "NIV" and "New International Version" are trademarks
registered in the United States Patent and Trademark Office by Biblica, Inc.™

WestBow Press books may be ordered through booksellers or by contacting:
WestBow Press
A Division of Thomas Nelson & Zondervan
1663 Liberty Drive
Bloomington, IN 47403
www.westbowpress.com
1 (866) 928-1240

Because of the dynamic nature of the Internet, any web addresses or links contained in
this book may have changed since publication and may no longer be valid. The views
expressed in this work are solely those of the author and do not necessarily reflect the
views of the publisher, and the publisher hereby disclaims any responsibility for them.

Any people depicted in stock imagery provided by Thinkstock are models,
and such images are being used for illustrative purposes only.
Certain stock imagery © Thinkstock.

ISBN: 978-1-5127-9644-5 (sc)
ISBN: 978-1-5127-9645-2 (hc)
ISBN: 978-1-5127-9643-8 (e)

Library of Congress Control Number: 2017911280

Print information available on the last page.

WestBow Press rev. date: 08/15/2017

This book was written for my beloved husband, our wonderful children, and our precious grandchildren, so that the miracles the Lord has done for our family will be known and not forgotten.

Our children have heard the stories in this book from their grandparents and from Dave and me. Now, our grandchildren, Lia, Beckett, Kyle, and Seth, whom we love so dearly, will have these stores in writing.

Only be careful, and watch yourselves closely so that you do not forget the things your eyes have seen or let them fade from your heart as long as you live. Teach them to your children and to their children after them.

—Deuteronomy 4:9 (NIV)

ACKNOWLEDGMENTS

Thank you to my wonderful, loving husband, Dave, who read and reread my manuscript and gave such good advice.

Thank you to my affirming, supportive daughter, Amy Beth, who helped me with all things technical.

Thank you to my dear, forever friend, Jackie, whose creative suggestions were invaluable.

CONTENTS

CHAPTER 1
Don't Shoot

When you and I wake up in the morning, we most likely do not think we are going to die that day, let alone be shot at. We get up; get ready; get going on our schedule for the day. And that was exactly how the day began for my father-in-law, Ralph Hanson, except that he was in a little house he had built for himself and his family on the barren, frozen tundra, sixty some miles north of Nome, Alaska. For you see, he and my mother-in-law, Alyce, had left the comfort and security of Minnesota for an incredibly harsh and arduous life near the Bering Sea, close to the Arctic Circle. They knew living there would be dangerous, but they did not expect the harrowing, life-threatening, close call Dave's dad experienced a few months after arriving in Nome, as described below.

My husband Dave's amazing father and equally remarkable mother were married in Minnesota and then took off on a train for Seattle on their honeymoon. That seems pretty standard, but what happened next is not standard at all. In fact, I think most of us couldn't imagine ever going on their kind of honeymoon, at least I can't.

From Seattle, Dave's parents, Alyce and Ralph Hanson, boarded a ship that would take them to one of the most northern points on the globe; it deposited them in Nome, Alaska, a bleak outpost at that time, on the Bering Sea. Wow, what a honeymoon! The most awe-inspiring part to me, though, is not that the newlyweds were going to Nome, but that they were going to stay—live—in that unbelievably cold, challenging place.

This, however, is where God's grace takes over and supersedes human reasoning. For, Alyce and Ralph had been called by the Lord to bring the good news about Jesus's love to the native people in tiny Eskimo villages, miles from Nome.

As they stepped from the ship on a chilly day in August, the sparse, unfamiliar landscape must have seemed forbidding and unwelcoming, but as was God's plan, a missionary couple stationed in Nome, who were dear friends of the Hansons from years past, met Dave's folks at the dock and brought them to stay at their home until Ralph could build a house for Alyce and himself in the hamlet of White Mountain, sixty miles northeast of Nome, where they would be headquartered.

All of this is astonishing to me (I live in a city that's in a warm climate), but now the story becomes even more exceptional.

Nome was cold, bare of trees (because it's on Alaska's arctic tundra), and dark several months of the year, due to being so close to the Arctic Circle. But at least it was a town. Still, the Lord hadn't called Dave's parents to minister in Nome; he had called them to go to small Eskimo villages, quite a distance from Nome, to share the Gospel. This, then, was going to be an even harsher life than life in Nome, which was at best, extremely severe.

Alyce and Ralph, though, were always open to following God's leading and thus began making plans and looking forward to their life in isolated White Mountain, the only village on the Seward Peninsula that was not situated by the ocean. Yet, though inland, it was on the banks of the Fish River, which was replete with various types of salmon and other fish varieties. (This resource would soon become greatly appreciated by the Hanson family, who were now so very far from the convenient food markets in Minnesota.)

Therefore, with much prayer, Ralph and his fellow missionary friend made the long trek to White Mountain by dogsled (the only way to traverse over ice and snow to Eskimo villages), lived with welcoming villagers, and spent months building a small home and beautiful little church in White Mountain.

Eventually, during the time Dave's folks served the Lord in Alaska, they also ministered to many in Golovin, approximately fifteen miles to the south of White Mountain, and in Council, about seventeen miles to the north. Golovin was situated at Golovin Bay, on the Seward Peninsula, where once a year, a ship would dock with supplies from Seattle, Washington. Dave's mom would have to make a shopping list for food and supplies that could last for a year! Can you imagine that? I can't. Driving to a market whenever I choose to do so is certainly a luxury I take for granted. (Please, Lord, help me to be more thankful.)

Life, as you can see, was very difficult and demanding for Alyce and Ralph, but also very rewarding, as many Eskimos heard the good news through them and came to have faith in Jesus as their Savior. Word spread to others through these new believers, and the little churches Ralph served in the villages began to grow, with more and more native people attending.

As Dave's parents settled increasingly into life in White Mountain and became close, trusted friends with the wonderful Eskimos who called it home, they began to hear snatches of conversations about a reclusive fur trapper who had come up from the Lower 48 years earlier. He lived alone, quite a ways from town, and wanted it that way; he had nothing to do with the villagers and made it clear by signs on his property: "NO TRESPASSERS!"

However, if you had known Dave's dad you would know he was one of the most undaunted people God ever created. Undaunted, courageous, visionary, and believing that with God, all things are possible: That was Ralph Hanson. So he determined to get to know the trapper and share the love of Jesus with him.

After finding out from villagers approximately where the hermit trapper lived, Dad set out to find him and do what no one else had been able to do: befriend him.

It was a cold, crisp, clear Alaskan day, near zero, with the sun gleaming off the blue-tinted ice as Ralph set off on his dogsled to find the trapper's cabin. Quite a distance from the village, with nothing else around for miles, Dave's dad finally spotted a cabin almost hidden by snowbanks.

"This must be what I'm looking for," Ralph decided. "It's generally in the vicinity the villagers mentioned."

A rough-hewn log cabin, with stairs, a porch, and a massive door, stood uninvitingly in a clearing, with two signs planted in front saying: "NO TRESPASSERS ALLOWED!"

Never to be deterred by what he considered imagined danger, or even actual danger, Ralph got off his dogsled and proceeded toward the cabin. When he got to the steps below the porch, as he related to us years later, Dad was stopped as though he had run into an invisible wall. He tried again to put his foot on the first step and was unable to do so. He had been stopped in his tracks and absolutely could not move forward. An invisible shield had been placed in his way that would not let him pass through.

As he stood there, frozen, Ralph knew it was not "something" that was stopping him; it was "Someone" who was protecting him. And he knew who that Someone was: the Lord Himself! Dave's dad did not know what he was being protected from, but he knew, most assuredly, that Jesus was protecting him. For that reason, he returned to his sled and traveled back to White Mountain.

Weeks later, the trapper came to the village for some supplies, and when the lone general store was out of what he wanted, he unleashed a shocking tirade:

"I hate this store, I hate this village, and I hate everyone who lives here!" he exclaimed. "I wish one of you would come out to my place because I have my shotgun rigged to blow your head off when you step on my porch!" He then exited in a rage and left those in the store in stunned silence, to put it mildly.

Word of his outburst spread quickly, and when Dad heard the story, he dropped to his knees and thanked God for saving his life. The Lord had dropped a protective shield to prevent him from stepping on that porch, saving him from certain death.

What a protecting, saving, loving God. He had protected Ralph and had given him many more years with his devoted family and precious Eskimo friends, who were so thankful he was alive and able to keep telling them about Jesus and His love for them.

"We love Him because He first loved us." (1 John 4:19 NKJV)

"And the LORD, He is the One who goes before you. He will be with you, He will not leave you nor forsake you; do not fear nor be dismayed." (Deuteronomy 31:8 NKJV)

"But, you, LORD, are a shield around me." (Psalm 3:3a NIV)

"The LORD protects and preserves them—they are counted among the blessed in the land—he does not give them over to the desire of their foes." (Psalm 41:2 NIV)

"I can do all things through Christ who strengthens me." (Philippians 4:13 NKJV)

CHAPTER 2
Run for Your Life

Rudolph. Santa's reindeer. Cute, sweet brown-eyed creatures that children love to pet at petting zoos around Christmas, right? Well, yes. In fact, I love reindeer and all God's creatures, and I work to protect them. However, you don't ever want to confront a life-extinguishing herd of thousands of rampaging reindeer. Yet that's exactly what happened to Dave's mom, Alyce Hanson, as you will see below.

In chapter 1, I tried to portray how amazing, courageous, and faith-filled Ralph Hanson, my husband's dad, was. I hope I succeeded. There was another Hanson, however, just as amazing, faith-filled, and possibly even more courageous in other meaningful ways. This person was Dave's mom, Alyce Hanson. She had been a successful, caring teacher in Minnesota when she met and fell in love with Ralph Hanson, a traveling evangelist and preacher for the Evangelical Covenant Church, a Christ-centered denomination with Swedish roots. Ralph loved Alyce at first sight and shared with her his belief that God was calling him to live with Eskimos near the Arctic Circle and share the love of Jesus with them.

Now, Ralph was used to cold, harsh weather, having grown up outside International Falls, Minnesota, in a farmhouse on the Rainy River, which divides Minnesota and Ontario, Canada. Alyce, too, was used to bitter weather, for she spent her early childhood in Ouray, Colorado, where her father and uncle owned and operated a gold and silver mine. Tragically, both Alyce's parents died when she was seven, and she was brought by her Uncle Gus to Minnesota, where she and her two young brothers were placed with, and grew up in different foster families. This made for a very sad childhood and difficult teenage years for a young girl.

As Alyce and Ralph's love deepened, they talked of marriage and prayed the Lord would tell them where He wanted them to serve Him. After several months, they both felt God had confirmed in them the fact that they were to go to Alaska, to help with the growing Covenant Church in Nome. Little did they know then that God had even more strenuous plans for them: ... living with and reaching out to the wonderful Eskimos in tiny hamlets, many miles from Nome. (Sometimes, the Lord only lets us see one step at a time, which is good.) Thus, Alyce and Ralph were married in a small chapel in northern Minnesota and left for their new life near the Bering Sea.

(I said I feel Alyce was even more courageous than Ralph in some ways, and I believe that. He was strong, hearty, healthy, and used to rough work on the family farm. She was a teacher, used to being in a classroom, and not a person who had 100 percent good health. Also, she was leaving a secure environment to live in a frozen, barren landscape, make a home there, and have children there. This would give most young women great pause for thought. For these reasons, I contend, Alyce was extremely courageous.)

After the long trip, first by train to Seattle, then by ship to Nome, Alyce and Ralph finally arrived at what was to be their new home. It couldn't have been easy for Alyce to adjust to this drastically different life. It was especially challenging because she had first one baby boy and then another, a few years after arriving in the severe atmospheric conditions and sparsely populated wilderness of Nome. Raising the boys, Paul and Dave, in a subarctic climate with long, frigid winters and short, cool summers, could not have been easy, either. Nevertheless, Alyce loved God, loved her husband, loved her children, and loved her life with all of them, so she prayed and persevered.

Besides family responsibilities, Dave's mom also taught Sunday school in the little White Mountain church and led a ladies' Bible study, through which she developed close relationships with many of the Eskimo women. Because of these friendships, Alyce and her friends would walk to each other's tiny homes during the short and greatly appreciated summer months, so their children could play together. The treat most asked for at these play times was a dessert only made in summer, when the mothers could go into areas outside the village, to pick berries with special baskets and combs. The berries were served over shaved ice, to the joy of the children: a true Eskimo delicacy.

One cool (but thankfully not cold) day in August, Alyce left Paul and Dave with their dad, who was working on a sermon, and went out to pick berries. She planned to serve some while still fresh and then preserve the rest to use during the winter months, when the only fruits and vegetables came from a can.

She had walked quite a ways from the village to where she knew the best berry bushes were; as she filled her basket, she heard an unfamiliar sound. Since only ground bushes grow on tundra (there are no trees for miles around Nome), sounds travels very quickly, and Alyce's ears were soon filled with an all-encompassing sound, coming closer and growing louder by the second. Then, suddenly, the ground began to shake; she was certain it was an earthquake, gathering steam.

But as she turned around, Alyce saw a sight that terrified her to the bone, much more terrifying than an earthquake! An enormous sea of reindeer was thundering toward her. Her first impulse, of course, was to run, but she knew she was powerless to get out of their way. The reindeer were stampeding, and this meant immediate death for anyone in their path!

Alyce realized there was no means of escape. The herd was too wide and galloping too fast. She dropped to her knees and began praying fervently, frantically, as she was sure she was going to be shredded to pieces by hundreds of hooves, as sharp as knives. What a horrific death that would be!

But just as the herd was about to trample her, the reindeer parted; they rushed by her at astounding speed, but on either side of her, not over her! Alyce was on her knees for interminable minutes while thousands of thundering deer parted perfectly, as though she weren't there. What a miracle! What an incredible, unbelievable answer to her prayers. What grace. Amazing grace!

Shaken, weak, and crying uncontrollably, she stood and made her way home, staggering on legs that would hardly hold her.

Ralph had felt the ground shake but had assumed it was a small earthquake, very common in Alaska, and had not given it a second thought. When Alyce appeared in their doorway, crying and shaking, Ralph gathered her in his arms and begged her to tell him what had happened. As she recalled her near-death experience and how Jesus had stepped in and parted the deer around her, Ralph pulled her even closer and thanked the Lord with a loud voice that God had saved his precious wife. Gratefulness permeated their little house that night and filled their appreciative hearts.

In later years, Dave's parents shared with us many of their Alaskan adventures and dangerous experiences, but the "parting of the reindeer" by Jesus, to save Alyce's life, was one of the most miraculous. That story has always reminded me of God's parting of the Red Sea for the Israelites fleeing Egypt, as told in the book of Exodus.

It has also reminded me to say, "Thank You, Lord, for saving Dave's mom by Your power, love, and grace."

"The LORD is my rock, my fortress and my deliverer; my God is my rock, in whom I take refuge." (Psalm 18:2a NIV)

"When I am afraid, I put my trust in you. In God, whose word I praise—in God I trust and am not afraid." (Psalm 56:3, 4a NIV)

"Jesus replied, 'What is impossible with man is possible with God.'" (Luke 18:27 NIV)

"Because of the LORD's great love we are not consumed, for his compassions never fail. They are new every morning; great is your faithfulness." (Lamentations 3:22, 23 NIV)

CHAPTER 3
Whirlwind Hanson

A blizzard with blinding snow that can overtake you and kill you! Whirling, deadly propeller blades that can shred you and kill you! Both of these deadly dangers were encountered by Dave's dad, and one of these potentially fatal experiences brought forth an invention that changed everything.

After several winter months on Alaska's Seward Peninsula, a crisis occurred that changed the way Ralph Hanson, my dear father-in-law, ministered to the tiny, extremely remote Eskimo villages of White Mountain, Golovin, Council, Elim, Solomon, and Unalakleet. The weather had been extraordinarily brutal, with weeks of subzero temperatures and blizzard upon blizzard. Ralph began to be especially concerned about one of the most distant villages because no one from that village had been seen in White Mountain for some time. (White

Mountain, where the Hansons lived, was definitely remote itself, being about sixty miles northeast of Nome, but in this wilderness, everything was relative; the other villages were even smaller and more outlying than White Mountain.)

Because of his concern for the Eskimos in the village no one had heard from in weeks, Dave's dad decided that when there was a break in the weather, he would ski to the village and bring them what supplies he could carry. (There were no roads from village to village on the frozen tundra; therefore, after arriving in White Mountain, Dad had made his own cross-country skis by taking wooden planks, forming them into skis and making his own poles, as well.)

On the first clear day, Ralph fully packed a backpack with supplies he thought the villagers might need, strapped on his skis, and took off. The trip would be 120 miles over ice and snow. I consider 120 miles by car a long trip. Can you imagine trekking 120 miles over barren, frozen tundra?

Another blustering storm formed before he could make it to the village, and Dave's dad had to ski thirty miles a day in critically dangerous conditions to reach his destination alive. Plunging through life-threatening whiteouts, subzero temperature, and Arctic winds like hurricanes almost took Ralph's life several times!

By the grace of God, however, and through the Lord's divine protection, Dad arrived at the village where he found, to his great relief, the people there were snowbound, but safe and well. After delivering his supplies, he returned home again a few days later with his life intact.

Most people would be terribly shaken by those near-death experiences, but Dave's dad's main concern was that it took so long and was sometimes almost impossible to reach the tiny villages far from Nome. His heart was with the Eskimos in all the villages, not just those in White Mountain, and he wanted to share the love of Jesus to those near and far. Unfortunately, the only way to travel at that time was by dogsled or skis, both slow and cumbersome, and that was the impetus leading to his historic decision.

He immediately began building two incredible vehicles that would enable him to travel over water and land from village to village in much less time and with some degree of safety. Necessity is indeed the mother of invention (or in this case, the father of invention).

Ralph first constructed a twenty-foot boat out of wood, and when finished, he mounted a four-cylinder aircraft engine on the back. (The engine was from a small plane that had crashed near the shore of Norton Sound. Dad unbolted the engine and also other parts he could use on his next projects.) This may have been the first time an airplane engine was anchored to the back of a boat, and though it made travel very fast, Ralph decided it was too unstable; he, therefore, eventually replaced the airplane engine with an Evinrude outboard engine.

Alyce and Ralph named the completed boat the *Evangel*; and of course, because Dave's dad had constructed it, the vessel was completely water worthy, and was used by Ralph and Alyce to go to some villages by water, such as from Golovin to Unalakleet. (According to Dave, there was a deck in the front of the *Evangel* with two small beds underneath, where he and Paul would go to stay out of wind and rain, and also to nap.)

Other villages, though, could only be reached over land, and Ralph became more and more vexed about the time he was spending skiing or dogsledding over ice and snow. This challenge brought out the creative, visionary, inventive side of Dave's dad; the result was the finished product Ralph called his "snow plane."

First, he built the main part out of wood and configured it like an airplane fuselage. This shell was made of rounded oak stakes, covered by stretched canvas, and next brushed with airplane dope (shellac). Then he mounted an abandoned Harley-Davidson "knucklehead" motorcycle engine on the nose of the snow plane's fuselage. Next, Ralph attached three large skis to his amazing invention, with enormous heavy steel brackets, using automotive-type suspension. Unbelievably, this truly incredible undertaking was finished in less than six months, in his spare time, and Dad was ready to roll.

Ralph later made four additional snow planes, each one more advanced than the former. Sadly, there had been several crashes of small aircraft in the greater Nome area in preceding years, the remains of which were still where they had crashed. For his succeeding snow planes, Dave's dad had unbolted an engine from one of the crashed airplanes and mounted it on his snow plane's cabin. Ralph's first snow plane was a "pull," with the engine mounted in the front. The next four were "pushes," the engine being affixed to the rear. Again, he may have been the first to create a snow plane, but Ralph Hanson was not constructing these machines for patents and profit; he was engineering and designing them to better minister to the Eskimos he respected, valued, and loved.

Flying over the frozen tundra in his snow plane at up to seventy-five miles per hour made it possible for Dad to visit Eskimos miles from White Mountain much more quickly and more often, to preach, teach, and share the good news with them that Jesus was alive and loved them absolutely and unconditionally.

It was on one of these trips in his new creation, the snow plane, that a mighty miracle occurred, one of the many, many miracles God showered on Dave's dad during his lifetime. It happened when Ralph was on his way from their home in White Mountain to the village of Council, about seventeen miles north. Snow had started falling as he ventured out, but that was the norm, since the White Mountain area received many feet of snow every year. Rain in the summer and then snow in the winter were just a part of everyday life ... nothing out of the ordinary. This day, however, proved not to be an ordinary day.

The snow, which initially had been falling softly and not heavily enough to even notice, suddenly began coming down in sheets. A severe Arctic storm had blown in off the Bering Sea and was overtaking the snow plane. Ralph carried on, undaunted as usual, but soon, Dave's dad was forced to stop suddenly, for he couldn't see at all. A whiteout was making visibility zero.

Dad's senses quickly became acute because he knew there was a deep, miles-long crevasse nearby, which would bring sure death if he were to fall into the abyss. (That had happened to some in the past during a blizzard.) Familiar guideposts along the way from White Mountain to Council had been obliterated by the wall of white, so there was no way for Ralph to know where the deadly chasm was, except to leave the snow plane and carefully feel his way along with his feet, taking small steps. He did this, carefully and slowly, trying to get his bearings in order that he could continue on his journey, even with zero visibility.

He reasoned that if he could find where the cavernous crevasse was and headed away from it, he would be traveling in the general direction of Council and safety. After just a few minutes of trying to find the edge of the canyon with his feet and hands, he touched the slope of snow surrounding the deep fissure. Terror and thankfulness combined as Dave's dad realized how close he had come to death. If he had kept going straight ahead, he would surely have gone over the edge, falling into the gaping hole with ice at the bottom. Now that Ralph knew he must change course, 180 degrees, he felt his way back to where he believed he had left his vehicle.

The blizzard continued to rage, with blankets of snow and howling winds, so Dad could not hear or see his snow plane. (The engine was still running.) Suddenly and dramatically, however, a miracle took place. Just as when Dad had been stopped from stepping foot on the trapper's porch, a wall once again dropped, and he could not move past it. He absolutely could not proceed through the invisible wall! Dad immediately knew without a doubt that Jesus was protecting him, and he stood perfectly still and prayed. (Later, he shared that he didn't know how long he had stood, immovable and praying, but at last the snow started to abate, and the winds calmed.)

Finally, when Ralph could see and hear, he was astounded: He was just inches from the snow plane's whirling propellers. He would have been sliced to bits by the knifelike blades if God had not slammed down an invisible, holy wall to stop him.

"Oh Lord, thank You! Thank You," was what Dad kept repeating as he climbed back into his machine and turned toward Council, for the Lord Himself had acted once again to save his life.

Dave's dad continued whirling across ice and snow in his snow planes for several more years. In fact, he was such a force, traveling from one village to another in his remarkable creations, that he was eventually known far and wide as "Whirlwind Hanson."

After Alyce and Ralph had been ministering in Alaska for almost six years, they had to leave, due to Alyce's poor health. When they bade goodbye to their dear friends, villagers who were like family to them, there wasn't a dry eye. The Eskimos in Nome and from all the outlying villages thanked Alyce and Ralph earnestly and profusely for coming to tell them that Jesus was real, was alive, and loved them beyond what they could imagine.

Dave's parents returned to the "Lower 48 States" where, after Alyce's health became stabilized, Ralph became the pastor of the Evangelical Covenant Church in Berkeley, California, for two years; subsequently, he was called to be the Executive Secretary of World Missions for the Evangelical Covenant Church of America. This meant he would be in charge of all the denomination's missionaries worldwide. What a challenge! Extraordinarily so. Dave's dad, though, had always been one to love a challenge and would seize an opportunity when he knew it was from the Lord.

The obstacles faced and overcome, the opened doors, and the remarkable accomplishments achieved during the nineteen years of Ralph's leadership as Executive Secretary of World Missions would be a book in itself, and maybe one day it will be. He had a heart for all the Covenant mission outreaches around the world, but I feel he left part of his heart in Alaska when they left.

Testimony to my belief that Dave's dad left part of his heart in Alaska is this: After leaving Alaska and becoming a pastor in Berkeley, California, Ralph took and passed the test to become a pilot, so he could fly the Covenant's mission plane. Consequently, he would fly this Stinson plane on his many return trips to Alaska, and became a pioneer in missionary aviation.

In addition, during his years as leader of World Missions for the Covenant Church, Dave's dad was instrumental in helping to: open a Children's Home (and later a High School) in Unalakleet, Alaska; a radio station called KICY in Nome; and, later in life, a radio station in Bethel, Alaska.

Dave's parents, Alyce and Ralph were an exceptional, courageous couple, totally dedicated to sharing the Lord's love with others. Ralph, as these stories illuminate, was also a one-of-a-kind adventurer, and even though he had left Alaska, adventure continued to follow him. Or should I say, he continued to follow adventure.

EPILOGUE

A story circulated in Nome and the surrounding areas after Dave's parents had had to leave due to Alyce's health, and this is how the tale went:

When Ralph had to leave Alaska, he had given his latest snow plane to a friend in Nome, knowing he would take good care of it and use it wisely. This was during World War II, and as the telling goes, United States Army personnel approached the new owner of the snow plane Dad had built and "commandeered" it. They said it was needed to use as a prototype in case the Japanese invaded Alaska from the Bering Strait. If that happened, they stated, copies of Hanson's snow plane would be manufactured to carry weapons and supplies to American soldiers, who would then be fighting Japanese soldiers on Alaskan soil. The Japanese invasion of Alaska never happened, thankfully, but the story of the need for Ralph Hanson's snow plane invention persisted. ...

(The LORD is speaking.)

"Be strong and courageous. Do not be afraid; do not be discouraged, for the LORD your God will be with you wherever you go." (Joshua 1:9b NIV)

"The LORD is my strength and my shield; my heart trusts in him, and he helps me." (Psalm 28:7a NIV)

"We wait in hope for the LORD; he is our help and our shield." (Psalm 33:20 NIV)

"Whether you turn to the right or to the left, your ears will hear a voice behind you, saying, 'This is the way; walk in it.'" (Isaiah 30:21 NIV)

CHAPTER 4
Watch Out for the Witch Doctor

When you hear the words "witch doctor," what comes to your mind? The villain in an adventure movie? Someone you wouldn't want to meet in a jungle? Or do you think witch doctors don't exist anymore? Well, they do exist; they have great power in some remote areas of the world, and Ralph Hanson went head-to-head with one, as you'll see when you read the adventure below.

Due to Alyce's ill health, the Hanson family moved to the "Lower 48 States," where Ralph pastored a church in Berkeley, California, before being chosen to be in charge of all the missionaries worldwide for the Evangelical Covenant Church of America. Since the headquarters of this denomination was in Chicago, Alyce, Ralph, Paul, and Dave moved to the Windy

City, right across the street from the church my immediate and extended family attended. I noticed the new boy, Dave, at once. He was the tallest, cutest, most active, and unforgettable boy I'd ever seen, and that has never changed.

Dave's dad, being a faith-filled visionary, began almost immediately to pray and plan for expanding the reach of Covenant missions to new places in the world. Therefore, after much prayer, and with God's leading, Ralph embarked with a missionary friend upon an extensive survey trip into Latin America. They traveled eighteen thousand miles and visited thirteen countries, splitting up at times to visit as many areas as possible. (The result of this expedition was the opening of Covenant missionary work in Ecuador, including building churches and eventually a high school.)

Dad, in later years, related to us many of his Latin American adventures, but one in particular has stayed in my mind above all others. After his initial foray with his missionary friend, Ralph returned to Latin America about a decade later, to see firsthand how the mission outreach had expanded, both in cities and in the jungle.

On this return trip, after visiting churches in towns and larger urban areas, Dave's dad said he wanted to travel to the headwaters of the Amazon River, which were inhabited, in some parts, by the Jivaro people, well-known for their head-hunting raids on others.

Never one to be afraid or dismayed by danger, Ralph asked specifically to visit a small church in the jungle, attended by some who had been head-hunters, but were now Christians whose lives had been changed by the love of Jesus. I'm sure Alyce, Paul, and Dave would have been more than a bit concerned, had they known their beloved husband and father was going to be in Jivaro territory.

However, as I've said, nothing ever seemed to frighten Dave's dad, not even the fact that two of his friends, Jim Elliot and Nate Saint, and three others had been killed two years before, as they tried to befriend the Auca Indians on a jungle beach in Ecuador. (There have been many inspiring books and movies about these men who died, including *Through Gates of Splendor*, by Elisabeth Elliot.)

As I stated earlier, of all the beyond remarkable adventures Dad related to us, the one I feel is the most astounding is the one he described in an essay he wrote for us, entitled, "My Long Weekend with the Jivaro Indian Head-hunters on the Head-waters of the Amazon River."

When Dave's dad and his guide began their expedition to find the Jivaro, they left Quito, the capital city of Ecuador, by traveling on a paved highway. This highway, though, eventually became a narrow road, winding through the Andes Mountains, with steep cliffs on the sides and the Amazon rainforest below. Then, after many miles of switchback curves, they threaded their way, precariously, down to the jungle floor, where the barely passable road turned into a dirt path that had been forged through the jungle rainforest.

The going was very tough, Dad recalled, but they finally came to a river, a tributary of the headwaters of the Amazon, and

Ralph's guide led him to a long, wooden canoe, which would take them the rest of the way to their destination.

To say the village they were heading to was isolated from the outside world would be an extreme understatement. To say danger lurked at every turn, from animals and humans, would be accurate. Ralph Hanson, though, was not only a man who deeply loved God, he also loved adventure and truly trusted the Lord to protect him. In this unpredictable, tenuous situation, he was in his element.

Finally, the guide maneuvered the canoe to a small beach on the river, where they disembarked and hiked up a path to two small houses made of materials gathered from the surrounding rainforest. The missionary couples who lived in these homes came out to see who had arrived and were thrilled to see Ralph Hanson, for missionaries everywhere loved him and so appreciated the heart he had for missions.

Inside, over food and drink, the couples shared what was happening in their lives, their ministry, and in the Jivaro community. Dave's dad learned than unlike other peoples, the Jivaroan families didn't live in villages; they lived far from each other in large, oval, one-room communal houses, also built from materials found in the jungle. A family and all their relatives lived in one home, near their farm, and in the general vicinity of the other families, but not in a village. The men joined together, however, in hunting parties, usually hunting animals (but sadly, sometimes hunting other people). The missionaries also disclosed that the Jivaro traditional religion was polytheistic, believing in many gods; they believed, too, that a person's soul was in the head and that a human head gave supernatural powers to the one who had taken it. This was the impetus for their head-hunting, along with their desire for revenge on other tribes.

People in other parts of the world have also been head-hunters, but apparently only the Jivaroan tribes are recorded as shrinking the heads of those they've beheaded.

Dave's dad already knew most of this information, but the sharing was greatly appreciated by all in that small home; and, as they talked and then prayed together, the missionaries and Dad focused on the problem of the local shaman, whom we would call the witch doctor. He was extremely powerful. Each large group of Jivaros had their own shaman, whom they looked to for healing and religious leadership, and they followed his directives regarding fighting and revenge. In other words, the witch doctor was their leader.

In addition, this powerful man was not happy about the fact that some in his area had become Christians and were now attending services in the little church built by the missionaries. They had been changed through their faith in Jesus and were no longer interested in fighting or revenge.

Not happy? Not at all. The witch doctor was not happy about Jivaros becoming Christians, and the couples voiced their concerns regarding what the shaman might do. If he gave the command, the Jivaro men who weren't Christians might slaughter the ones who were, their families, and the missionaries. They were at his mercy. There were no police stations to call or 911 numbers to dial. They were a little band of Christian believers in the rainforest jungle, surrounded by possible headhunters. In spite of all this, they knew they were not alone. Jesus was with them, and His protective angels were encompassed around about them.

The next day, Saturday, was also filled with conversation, laughter, breaking bread together, and praying. Then, it was Sunday, time to go to church.

Dad had been asked by the missionaries to preach and also play a few songs on the guitar at their cherished church in the jungle. Ralph was honored and of course said yes, being assured that one of the missionaries would translate his words. Everyone knew there would be a great attendance at the Sunday service because Dave's dad was a novelty; besides those Jivaros who were now believers, many non-Christians would come out of curiosity.

With much prayer and preparation, Dad looked forward to proclaiming the gospel of Christ's love to the dear people nestled in the rainforest, at the headwaters of the mighty Amazon River. There was also a bit of apprehension on the part of the missionaries because they knew the witch doctor had surely heard about the stranger's arrival and that he was going to be talking in the Christians' meeting place on Sunday. They knew, too, and shared with Ralph that the witch doctor would consider the stranger an enemy and could summon his fighters to attack the church.

Never to be stopped by danger, Dave's dad just prayed fervently and took off for church with his friends, early Sunday morning.

It was very hot and extremely humid as the Jivaros streamed into the little church. In fact, because so many more than usual arrived, there was eventually standing room only when the service started! Ralph began by playing the borrowed guitar and singing: "I Love to Tell the Story of Jesus and His Love," and "What a Friend We Have in Jesus." He then began his message.

So touched was Dad by the upturned, attentive faces before him, he almost didn't notice someone who came in late and stood alone in the back. A moment later, though, Ralph stopped midsentence and stared, as he realized the man who had just entered was the witch doctor. Dave's dad took a deep breath and prayed for strength, as he wondered if there were men outside, ready to attack. (He told us later that when he prayed, he felt a surge of power come over him, and he knew the Holy Spirit was filling the room and Jesus was standing right beside him.)

As the awareness that the shaman (witch doctor) was in the back began to ripple though the church, tensions rose, and the fear was palpable! In spite of the threat, Dad carried on, speaking more confidently than ever about the love of Christ, and how accepting Jesus as your Savior will fill you with peace and joy. Then, to Ralph's relief, and also sadness), toward the end of the sermon, the witch doctor got up and quietly left.

Yet the Lord was powerfully present in the small jungle church that day, as many formerly hostile Jivaros, who had come just to see the stranger preach, believed in Jesus and became Christians through hearing the sermon by Dave's dad.

Ralph never heard, in the ensuing years, whether the witch doctor came to believe in Christ, but he did hear that he was no longer threatening those who did believe. And I'm sure, knowing Dad, that he continued to pray, until the day he went to heaven, for that shaman at the headwaters of the Amazon River.

"The LORD your God in your midst, the Mighty
One, will save." (Zephaniah 3:17a NKJV)

"The LORD is good, a stronghold in the
day of trouble." (Nahum 1:7a NKJV)

"Whoever dwells in the shelter of the Most High
will rest in the shadow of the Almighty. I will say
of the LORD, 'He is my refuge and my fortress,
my God, in whom I trust.'" (Psalm 91:1, 2 NIV)

"God is our refuge and strength, an ever-
present help in trouble." (Psalm 46:1 NIV)

CHAPTER 5
To Live or Die

Some things in life are hard. Some things in life are heart-breaking. Some things in life, we just don't understand. That's where we need, more than ever, the anchor of trust.

Ralph Hanson's adventures and near-death experiences continued. Actually, as Executive Secretary of World Missions for the Evangelical Covenant Church, he may have needed the Lord's protective miracles even more than when he was a missionary in Alaska. In his new position, he was often in extremely dangerous situations and places, for he traveled to distant outposts on many continents, assisting missionaries who were bringing food, health services, education, and the good news of Jesus's love to the peoples God had called them to serve.

One of these dangerous situations occurred in China.

Civil war had been raging for a year between the Communists, led by Mao Zedong, and the Chinese government. The national government had more troops and weapons and controlled more territory, but the Communists were strong in the northern parts of China and were gaining support in the villages there. This was the background when Covenant missionaries in China began writing home to the United States, saying they were worried about the growing power of the Communists. They reported there were rumors that Mao and his troops were taking over more and more villages and were moving closer to where the Covenant mission station was located.

The missionaries sent letters to Dave's dad to inform him of their concerns; they also wrote to friends and family members in our small Swedish section of the city of Chicago, called North Park. (The headquarters of the Covenant Church, their college, seminary, and hospital were, and still are, located the in North Park community.)

The missionaries were not writing because they wanted to leave China; they had no intention of doing so, but they wanted Dave's dad to know what they were seeing and hearing. Most of all, they asked for prayers for their safety and that all would be settled peacefully in China.

Never one to sit idly by while things happened, Ralph made plans to go to China to see the dangers for himself and decide if he should call the missionaries home to the United States and out of harm's way. Soon, then, Dad took off on a flight from Chicago to China, holding a glimmer of hope that China's civil war would calm down.

When he arrived, the missionaries, all dear friends of Dave's dad, were overjoyed to see their courageous, capable, compassionate boss; they were extremely relieved that they could now communicate with him face-to-face.

As they shared their fears about the Communists' gaining ground and the national government crumbling, Ralph absorbed the reality of the situation. He and the missionaries prayed together, read the Bible together, ate together, and spoke late into the night about the impending crisis looming over China: a Communist takeover of the country. This would mean sure persecution and possible death for Christian missionaries.

After several days of listening to and praying with his missionary friends, Dave's dad made the decision that all the Covenant missionaries in China should go back to the United States until the civil war ended, hopefully with the national government intact and the Communist forces retreating. Ralph's friends at the mission station knew this was the correct decision, but their hearts were broken as they planned to pack up and leave the Chinese people they loved so deeply and the country to which God had called them.

As Dad was preparing to leave and return home, three of the missionaries (two nurses and a doctor) came to him and said that after much prayer, they had decided they did not want to fly back to the States with the others, who were going soon, because they were registered to attend an important medical conference in a few weeks, a day away by bus, sponsored by several denominations. It would be a wonderful opportunity to network with other Christian medical personnel, they persuaded, who could be helpful partners with them when the civil war was over and they could return to China. The missionaries also promised they would keep a low profile, not travel anywhere else except the conference, and would bundle their belongings for the return trip to the United States as soon as they returned from the medical meeting.

Dave's dad reluctantly agreed because he understood their hearts and desire to help the Chinese people, no matter what the cost, for he had felt the same way in Alaska. Therefore, amid parting prayers, embraces, and "God bless you," Dad departed and made his way home to Chicago.

The news that arrived to the North Park community not long after Dave's dad had returned from China was crushing, devastating, and absolutely heart-wrenching. On the way to the medical conference, the bus carrying Ralph's dear friends, the doctor and both nurses, was stopped by Communist soldiers.

They were pulled off the bus and asked, "Are you a Christian?"

When they, one by one, replied, "Yes," they were shot and left along the roadside to die. It still brings tears to my eyes to think of it.

As news of these tragic deaths spread, people across our country wept, including my parents and grandparents, and, of course, Dave's parents, whose hearts were broken. His dad was especially devastated, for these martyrs were his close friends and fellow workers. Alyce realized, too, that her dear Ralph had, once again, been close to danger, which was his choice, as one who went where the Lord sent him.

"The eternal God is your refuge, and underneath are the everlasting arms." (Deuteronomy 33:27a NKJV)

(Jesus is speaking.)

"He said to them, 'Go into all the world and preach the gospel to all creation.'" (Mark 16:15 NIV)

"For this God is our God for ever and ever; he will be our guide even to the end." (Psalm 48:14 NIV)

"Jesus answered him, 'Truly I tell you, today you will be with me in paradise.'" (Luke 23:43 NIV)

CHAPTER 6
What a Shock

Think of receiving a shock. Do you remember a time when you heard unwelcome news, or when something totally unexpected happened? Well, those are shocks, to be sure, but there are other types of shocks, as well.

Growing up in the Swedish enclave of North Park in the city of Chicago was an idyllic childhood, except for one thing. The idyllic part was that I lived with my loving parents (Marie and Dave Carlson) and my wonderful brother, Tom, in our own brick bungalow. Tom and I also had two sets of grandparents, and aunts and uncles, nearby, as an integral part of our childhood. The love and affirmation we received was what every child would want. (There was an added joy too, regarding our brick bungalow. We had an apple tree in our backyard: a wonderful anomaly in the midst of a city.)

There was, though, as I said, one exception to my otherwise happy young years: I kept coming down with painful and serious strep infections, which led to even more serious complications, such as rheumatic fever. My doctor finally sat my parents down when I was thirteen and stated firmly, "If you want your daughter to stay alive, and I know you certainly do, you need to move to Florida or California."

Wow, my poor parents. Their lives were imbedded in the North Park community. They had lived there all their lives; their extended families were there; their childhood friends were there; their beloved church was there; and, my father's hard-earned and excellent job was in downtown Chicago. In spite of all this, my dear parents sold our wonderful home, and we packed up and moved to California.

I'm sure I'll never know the depth of what my mom and dad gave up when we made that move, but the older I became, the more I understood. They made sacrifices for me because they loved me with the love of devoted parents and with the love of Jesus flowing through them.

However, though the move was traumatic for all of us, especially for my precious father, who had an extremely difficult time finding a job, the Lord had plans for us in this new place, Los Angeles, as He always does.

Jesus was with us as we adjusted to life in the California sun: I became, and continued to stay, healthy; Mom went back to being a nurse at a Covenant Church retirement home; Dad finally found a job; and, we all settled into the Evangelical Covenant Church in Eagle Rock. Later, we became members of a new Covenant Church in La Crescenta, much closer to our home.

The La Crescenta church was a beautiful A-frame nestled at the foot of the San Gabriel Mountains, filled with caring people and led by Christ-filled pastors. It was in these lovely, inspiring surroundings that my mom, brother, and I learned of another family miracle.

It was New Year's Eve, and at that time many churches held a "Watch Night Service" on New Year's Eve, from 11 p.m. until midnight. (Maybe some churches still do.) It was a time when we gathered to give testimonies and pray during the hour before the new year was rung in.

On one particular New Year's, when I was in high school, I was actually not in the sanctuary but in the kitchen with my mom, Marie, helping to plate and arrange refreshments that had been lovingly prepared by members of our church family. Therefore, unfortunately, Mom and I missed the service and the always-uplifting personal stories people shared of how Jesus had helped them throughout the year.

Just as we heard fireworks going off in the neighborhood, signaling the clock had struck midnight, church members began streaming into the fellowship hall to partake of the sandwiches, casseroles, and desserts my mom and I had placed on the buffet table. (In a church with a Swedish heritage, there was always delicious food for every occasion.) As we went back into the kitchen to refresh the platters, Mom and I were followed by several friends who began talking excitedly over each other:

"Marie," one said, "you must be so thankful your husband didn't die in the amazingly close call!"

"Why didn't you tell us Dave had been through such a frightening experience?" another one asked. Others followed with:

"We were all shocked when he gave his testimony tonight and told about his narrow escape."

"He actually turned pale when talking about it."

"Thank the Lord that Dave's alive!"

To say Mom and I were astounded would be an understatement. First of all, my dad never gave a testimony. He had a deep, solid faith, and had since childhood, but my dad wasn't one to openly share his feelings. (David Albert Emanuel Carlson was very Scandinavian in this regard: deep faith, quietly lived out as an example of God's love.)

Adding to our astonishment was the fact that neither my mom nor I knew anything about a close call or a narrow escape.

I said nothing, and my mom managed to sputter, "Yes, we are very, very thankful," and we then began carrying more food to the tables, so we could compose ourselves.

What in the world were these friends talking about? We couldn't fathom it, but you can imagine it was the first question we asked Dad when we got into the car to drive home later that night.

"What did you share in the church service? What happened that almost killed you? Why didn't you tell us?"

My dad looked from one of us to the other, took a deep breath, and started talking:

"Well," he began, "at work, another man and I were given the assignment of fixing an electrical generator that had started sparking, so we carried our tools and long ladder to where the problem was. The electricity to the generator had been turned off when the sparking began," he continued, "so when we got to the defective generator, we took out our tools and grabbed our ladder. Our procedure always was to set the ladder carefully against the affected wires, climb up and fix the problem, but this time, we both let go of the ladder, and it fell against the wires."

Wiping his hand across his eyes, Dad paused for a moment and then said softly, "The second we let go and the ladder touched the wires, flames shot out like a blowtorch, and we realized the electricity had *not* been turned off! It had shot down the ladder and into the ground. If we had been touching the ladder, as we usually did, we would both have been electrocuted."

He stopped talking because his voice was shaking, and I could tell he was trying to hold himself together.

I started crying, and Mom just whispered, "Dave ... sweetheart ... Dave," and took his hand.

My brother and I sat in sober silence, and then, we all in our own way said, "Thank You, Lord! Thank You, Lord, for saving him."

It still makes me weak to think of how close we came to losing my beloved, special, remarkable, loving father, who would do anything for us (and always did). I'm beyond grateful to Jesus for letting us have Dad for almost forty more years.

My dad was such an example on earth of how much our heavenly Father in heaven loves us.

I love you so much, Dad, and still miss you every day.

"For I know the plans I have for you," declares the LORD, "plans to prosper you and not to harm you, plans to give you hope and a future." (Jeremiah 29:11 NIV)

"And we know that in all things God works for the good of those who love him, who have been called according to his purpose." (Romans 8:28 NIV)

"Give thanks to the LORD, for he is good; his love endures forever." (1 Chronicles 16:34 NIV)

"For he will command his angels concerning you to guard you in all your ways; they will lift you up in their hands, so that you will not strike your foot against a stone." (Psalm 91:11, 12 NIV)

CHAPTER 7
The Walls Came Tumbling Down

The Lord is always watching over us, caring for us, and making "all things work together for good" (even things that are not good). Though we know this is true, sometimes we cannot see how things are working together until we look back, from a distance. In light of this, I think the chapter below will make you laugh, cry, and say, "Thank You, Lord, that Lee and Dave are alive."

When Dave and I were in college, it was all the rage to go to Europe for the summer. You could fly extremely inexpensively on a group rate with others from your school, and seeing as the dollar was very strong then, your money went a long, long way. Even so, we would not have been able to afford such a trip if it hadn't been for the fact that though Dave was still in college (due to a stint in the California National Guard), I had graduated and was teaching English in a small Christian high school. Even that wouldn't have helped enough to enable us to save for a trip to Europe; however, the school had a few (13) resident students, and that is what saved the day (or to be more exact, the trip) for us.

It happened that the dorm parents who were supposed to be caring for the thirteen dorm students were having a hard time dealing with and controlling their charges, so the principal asked if Dave and I would consider taking over their positions.

Wow! We had hit the jackpot. Being dorm parents meant having our own apartment, with the rent and utilities paid for by the school. This was the perfect solution for saving money in order to go to Europe. How hard could it be, we reasoned, to be in charge of one boy, living in the apartment above us, and twelve girls in the building behind us?

Well, the operative words were "in the building behind us." Knowing what twelve high school girls were doing when we weren't even on the same premises was challenging, to put it mildly, but worth it, for we were able to save enough to spend the summer in Europe: the chance of a lifetime!

We also had to sell our much-loved Austin Healy Sprite, but we knew it was necessary and then decided it would be smart to order a car in the United States before we left and pick it up at the factory in Germany. We could use it for our travels in Europe, instead of spending money on trains, and also have the car sent back to the US for us to have at home. Dave is a car guy, and this idea seemed perfect.

So we flew to London on a low-cost, student-fare group ticket, went by boat to Germany, and picked up our Karmann-Ghia convertible, right at the factory. Everything was going according to plan, and we were loving every minute. (Plans were going to change, however, but, of course, we had no idea what was coming.)

Being in Europe for three months and living on $5 a day (yes, we did that) is a book in its own right, but even so, the first month was fairly uneventful and full of memorable sights, sounds, and moveable feasts. (We had many picnics of bread, cheese, wine, and sumptuous little tarts.)

Before we left Los Angeles, I had made an itinerary of where we would be and given a copy to my folks, in La Crescenta, and mailed a copy to Dave's parents, who were in Chicago. (In those days, you could pick up your mail at every American Express office in Europe, which we always did, standing in a long line of college kids, all waiting to hear from home. That was a great and much appreciated service provided by American Express.)

We had been staying right on schedule, following our itinerary, when we rolled into Nice, on the French Riviera, one hot day in July. We usually stayed in youth hostels, which were often not great but always cheap. Once in a while, we would splurge and find an inexpensive, charming little hotel or bed and breakfast, as a special treat. This day, however, we asked directions and headed to the hostel in Nice. The manager, a rather surly woman, said we needed to come back at five o'clock; they didn't give out rooms until then.

We told her we'd be back, and meantime, because it was such a hot day, we'd go to the beach and enjoy the Mediterranean Sea. Not a bad way to spend an afternoon: hanging out at the beach in Nice! (Little did we know what this day at the beach was going to set in motion.)

Not ever having been on a major trip before, I didn't know much about packing, to put it mildly. Students in the know brought a backpack to Europe. I, on the other hand, brought five suitcases. Being gone three months, I reasoned, necessitated bringing all the clothes I owned. Therefore, I packed dressy clothes, casual clothes, cold weather clothes, hot weather clothes, my "going away on our honeymoon" clothes, and of course, a bathing suit. That day in Nice, I needed a bathing suit, so we changed in the youth hostel's restroom and took off for the beach.

The thermometer was soaring, as it always does in July on the French Riviera; thus, being by the water, where it was a bit cooler, was a welcome respite from the heat. (Many restaurants and shops closed every afternoon from 2 to 4:30 p.m., due to the temperature, so we weren't missing much in the town.)

After lounging by the Mediterranean for several hours, Dave and I leisurely walked back to our car, completely relaxed, but a bit sun-burned. That was when, to our astonishment and horror, we discovered disaster had struck!

While we were cooling off at the beach, thieves had slashed the top of our convertible and stolen all our belongings, and I mean *all*. My many suitcases and Dave's few were gone! In addition to the clothes we'd brought to last us for three months, our passports, American Express Travelers Cheques, and cameras were also in the car.

What a hard way to learn a lesson: Never leave anything in a convertible. Not only was everything we'd brought from home stolen, but our little Karmann-Ghia's top had been destroyed. I said above that we were horrified, but that's much too mild a word. Stunned, shocked, and staggered are more to the point. And to make matters worse, we had two months left until we again boarded the plane for home.

As I remember, I was in tears, and Dave was furious, neither of which were going to help our situation. Finally, some locals, who felt sorry for our plight, suggested we go to the police station to see if they could offer any assistance. That sounded like as good an idea as any, so we asked directions and headed towards the Poste de Police.

It was 4:30 p.m. when we reached the police station; fortunately, the main detective was still on duty and ushered us into his small, very hot, and very stuffy office. He spoke little English, so I had to struggle with my college French and an English-French dictionary to explain what had happened and what had been stolen.

He was pleasant and sympathetic but wanted to know every single item, no matter how insignificant, that had been in our suitcases: every single item. So we sat in a 90 degree room, with perspiration dripping down the inspector's face, as he wrote down in detail every article we had lost, including our Bible.

(He did look up when I said, "Bible," raised his eyebrows, and smiled. I guess he was not used to tourists reporting stolen Bibles.)

When I had finished with our exhaustive list, the detective sat back, cleared his throat, and then gave, in halting English, some very unwelcome news.

"I cannot," he started, then paused, and finally continued, "I cannot get back your things."

There was silence on our part, complete silence, for reality was sinking in. We were going to be in Europe for two more months with no clothes, no money, and no passports. What a total nightmare, disaster!

Then, though, sensing we were becoming fairly distraught, the inspector added, "But, listen." We stared at him intently as, mainly in French but in some English, he told us three astounding facts: The managers of the youth hostel we were staying at were Communists; they often had accomplices who followed and robbed tourists the managers said had nice clothes and money; and most importantly, they sometimes dumped what they didn't want up in the mountains above Nice.

To say we were shocked is an understatement, but we had nothing to lose, so Dave and I bade a hasty goodbye to the Poste de Police and, with the help of our Michelin map, began to wend our way up the mountain road behind the city. Of course, we had no doubt this was a fool's errand, but we wound around and around, higher and higher, till we could see the beautiful Mediterranean far below.

After several hopeless hours, as we were about to give up, an astonishing miracle happened. There in a heap, off to the side of the narrow road, was a large pile of open suitcases and debris, scattered under trees in the woods. As we drew closer, to our utter amazement, we saw that some of the wrecked suitcases were ours. They had been flung on top of many others, making clear the truth of the inspector's statement: "Sometimes the thieves dump what they don't want up in the mountains above Nice."

Searching desperately through the trash to find anything familiar, we soon realized that none of our belongings were there. Disappointed and dirty, we started to leave when Dave spied what looked like more rubbish farther from the rest. We walked over and, unbelievably, in the pine needles, were our passports and my camera.

All we could say was, "Thank You, Lord. Thank You. Thank You."

Our clothes were gone. Oh well. We could pick up a few things in town. No suitcases to worry about might be a blessing in disguise. Getting my camera back was a gift because we had a month of pictures on it. But our passports? Finding them was like finding pure gold. So excited and relieved by this were we that we put aside the fact that we still had no money and no place to stay.

Still, the truth of a matter has a way of reasserting itself, and on the way back down to Nice, reality once again set in; the reality was that we had three major problems: Our traveler's checks had been stolen, it would soon be dark, and we needed a place to sleep; plus, our car needed a new convertible top. All this was more than a bit overwhelming.

I solved the first problem in a rather unorthodox manner. When Dave and I got back to the city, I knocked on apartment doors, explaining in my very limited French, that we had been robbed and needed a place to stay. After many attempts, the grandmother of one family took pity on our plight and took us in. Whew!

The second problem was solved by our going to the American Express office the next day, where we found, to our tremendous relief, that they would replace *all* our stolen checks because Dave had kept a meticulous record of the numbers on the checks. (The actor's words in the commercial regarding American Express Traveler's Cheques were true: "Don't leave home without them.") Again, we said, "Thank You, Lord!"

Dave also solved the third, and last major problem, by finding an auto repair shop that would order and install a new top on our car. It was a blessing and a reassurance to have these challenges behind us, and we were able to actually relax a bit and enjoy the ambiance and delicious tastes of the French Riviera, all still, shockingly, on $5 a day.

There was only one hitch in all these now positive happenings (which, at the time, we viewed as just a change in plans, not a problem). This was the fact that waiting for the new convertible top to arrive from Germany put us a week off our schedule and, hence, one week off on the itinerary given to both sets of parents so they would know where we were. We hadn't wanted to worry them; consequently, we hadn't written home about our robbery and being a week behind on our route across Europe.

Dave and I felt no news, except good news, was better, but what we hadn't counted on was this: Somehow, the Nice police report concerning our being robbed had been picked up by the Associated Press, and Dave's parents, much to their horror, read a story in the *Chicago Tribune* about our theft. They, of course, immediately called my parents in California, and now there were two sets of extremely worried parents. And here we thought we were sparing them!

In addition to not knowing we had solved the problems of no money and a damaged car, our parents also didn't know we were now one week behind schedule on the itinerary we had given them. This, as it turned out, would soon cause them far more anguish and anxiety than news of the robbery had, as you will see.

After our delay in Nice, Dave and I set off, with a new convertible top on our car, for the glories of Florence and the history of Rome, both which were beyond anything we could have imagined.

While in Rome, we went to the Italian consulate and obtained permission to enter Yugoslavia. (This was in 1963, when Tito was in power as the president of Yugoslavia and it was part of the Soviet Union, behind the Iron Curtain. However, if you received a special dispensation in Rome, you could travel into that country for a limited amount of time.)

Also, when I was planning our itinerary, months before we left on our trip, I found out that Americans having the courage to foray behind the Iron Curtain into Yugoslavia usually went to the city of Skopje, in the area of ancient Macedonia, because it was a fascinating city that welcomed tourists. The only stipulation was that outsiders were told to stay at the approved hotel, located on the main square of Skopje. This was where all the international travelers stayed and was where we planned to stay.

Now, back to our traversing the magnificent, captivating, mesmerizing Italy. Leaving Rome, we wended our way to the jewel in the crown, Venice, and then on to Trieste, sitting on the edge of the cobalt-blue Adriatic. We splurged that night and stayed in a hotel, rather than a hostel, and I'll never forget the view from our balcony of the sparkling, clear Adriatic Sea, like a mass of twinkling blue stars.

In the midst of the beauty and peace, however, was the disquiet Dave and I both felt about going behind the Iron Curtain the next day. We knew others did it, and our papers were all in order, but still, the free world and Communist world were in the middle of a Cold War, and even though it had seemed like an excellent thing to do when we discussed our trip, the reality of going into Yugoslavia was now settling in.

The next morning, we arose at four o:clock, while it was still dark outside, and took leave of our hotel by five. We needed to get a very early start, because Skopje is 650 miles from Trieste.

Since we didn't want to stay anywhere along the route, we needed to make the drive in one fell swoop, and we knew we could. By leaving this early, we calculated we would arrive at the international hotel in early evening, which would be fine.

We were expecting trouble at the Italian-Yugoslavia border crossing, which unnerved us a bit; thus, we were both relieved when the papers that had been stamped by the Yugoslavian official in Rome worked like a charm. We sailed across the border without a hitch.

Because Dave and I were anxious to arrive in Skopje and the hotel where other American and European tourists would be staying, we had bought food and water in Trieste to have in the car so we could just move along and only stop for gas. The scenery was beautiful, and the towns we passed through were quaint and very Old World, with charming houses and small farms, but we began to notice one thing that stuck out: All the women were wearing black.

Now, we had become used to seeing many older women in Spain, France, and Italy wearing black, but here, the women of all ages were wearing black. At first, we thought it was the cultural tradition of a certain area, yet since we saw this everywhere as we continued our drive, our curiosity was piqued.

Finally, in a larger town where we stopped to get gas, I found someone who spoke a little English and asked him why all the women were wearing black. He looked at me, shocked, and tears filled his eyes.

"Do you not know?" he stammered. "Do you not know? Skopje has had an earthquake. It is destroyed!"

With tears streaming down his face, he walked away, leaving me stunned and speechless.

Dave was also beyond shocked when I got back in the car and cried, "Turn around. There's been a horrible tragedy. An earthquake destroyed Skopje. We've got to get back to Trieste!"

Our return ride to Italy was mainly silent, as we contemplated the horror of what had happened and the nightmare of what must be happening in the aftermath.

How could we not have known about the earthquake, we asked each other, soon realizing it was because we had not read a newspaper nor watched TV in our hotel in Trieste because we didn't understand Italian.

Then, another realization dawned on us: We would have been there when the earthquake hit! If it hadn't been for the robbery and destruction of our convertible top, which put us behind on our travel schedule, we would have been in Skopje when the earthquake struck! Just the thought of how close we had come to death made us take very deep breaths.

Dave pulled over to the side of the road so we could gather our thoughts and calm down. We looked at each other and then both whispered, "Thank You, Jesus. Thank You for protecting us. Thank You, and please, please help those who are injured, suffering, and grief-stricken in Skopje. Please put Your arms around them."

Solemnly, we made our way back to the hotel in Trieste, praying as we went.

What Dave and I didn't know, and didn't find out until we returned to Italy, was the unimaginable extent of death and destruction caused by the earthquake. It had been a 6.9 quake; the epicenter was under Skopje's town square; the city had been destroyed; and over a thousand people had died, with three to four thousand injured. That last fact was horrific beyond belief!

Realizing the scope of the catastrophe brought home to us once again how the earthquake had nearly taken our lives. The hotel where tourists stayed was at the town square and had crumbled like it was made of matchsticks. What an unbelievable tragedy for Skopje, all who were there, and Yugoslavia! (Whenever we think of this, even all these years later, it is very sobering. We don't know why we were spared. It is not something one can understand. Nonetheless, we thank God for His mercy and continue daily to appreciate, to our core, that we are alive.)

The next day, after the shock had settled into us, Dave and I began thinking about where we were and how our schedule had, this time tragically, been changed again. Then, all at once, it finally registered in our minds that our poor parents would think we had been in Skopje the day of the earthquake, in the hotel that went down. That's what our itinerary said, and they didn't know we had spent extra time in Nice because of the robbery!

Calling them quickly from the hotel, we assured them we were alive and well, and amid tears and "Thank You, Jesus," we told them we loved them and promised to do a much better job of keeping in touch and letting them know we were okay.

The rest of our trip was also exciting, eventful, and full of additional adventures, too many to enumerate here, but the Lord was with us then, everywhere we went, as He is now. Thanks be to God.

"Now to him [Jesus] who is able to do immeasurably more than all we ask or imagine." (Ephesians 3:20a NIV)

"For the LORD will be your confidence, and will keep your foot from being caught." (Proverbs 3:26 NKJV)

(The LORD is speaking.)

"Do not fear, for I have redeemed you; I have summoned you by name; you are mine. When you pass through the waters, I will be with you; and when you pass through the rivers, they will not sweep over you." (Isaiah 43:1b–2a NIV)

"But I trust in your unfailing love; my heart rejoices in your salvation. I will sing the LORD's praise, for he has been good to me." (Psalm 13:5, 6 NIV)

CHAPTER 8
Meeting the Mafia

Think *The Godfather*, "The Sopranos," and "Mad Men." Frightening groups of people, all. Well, Dave and I accidently had a brush with some men from the Mob and barely escaped with our lives. At the beginning of the last chapter, I said that after reading it, you might want to say, "Thank You, Lord, that Lee and Dave are alive." You may want to say the same words after reading this chapter.

Following our truly once-in-a-lifetime trip to Europe, Dave and I returned home by flying again with a group from his university. Also, as we'd done three months earlier, in order to get from Los Angeles to New York City, we arranged for a "drive-a-car" to drive back to California.

This way, we would drive a car across the country, at no cost to us, for someone who needed a vehicle transported. We'd even be reimbursed by the owner when we delivered the car to the address, somewhere in Los Angeles County. It was a "win-win"; and, for that reason, after we deplaned, one very hot September day in New York, we grabbed a cab and went immediately to the drive-a-car agency.

It was a steamy, stuffy office, three flights up, and the man at the one desk seemed nervous, as well as hot. He kept wiping his forehead with a handkerchief and said without looking up, "I only have one car left, and it has a stipulation with it. But it's all I've got, so if you want it, it's yours." Dave asked what the stipulation was, and the man replied, "You are forbidden to open the trunk."

That seemed a strange directive, but then if the owner had valuables in the trunk that could be broken if rearranged, maybe it wasn't so out of line. We agreed we would not use the trunk and then asked what kind of car we would be driving.

"It's a Cadillac Coupe deVille," the now heavily perspiring man informed us.

"Wow," Dave exclaimed. "Quite a car. But not one we want because of the gas it will take to drive across the whole country."

"Well, it's the only one I have," was the answer.

So we took the car and started the almost-three-thousand-mile trek home.

Our nonstop journey from NYC to LA, with a one-night stopover in Chicago to see Dave's parents, was uneventful, except for one fairly hysterical event. Since we were feeling rather grimy from our flight and then immediate takeoff in the Coupe deVille, we decided to clean up a bit during our next stop for gas.

Dave was going to shave, so he took his large, vinyl tote bag and zipped it open to retrieve his shaving kit. Much to his shock, the bottle of liquid detergent we had brought with us had opened, and it had spread over everything in the small suitcase!

Dave took all items out, grabbed a hose attached to the gas station, and began to hose off the inside of his bag. This seemed like a good idea at the moment; however, there were two major problems.

First of all, there was a whole bottle of detergent in the tote, and second, there was a long, three-foot-deep ditch nearby, being dug by workers for a sewer line. As Dave power-hosed his suitcase, suds began foaming up and out of the tote, spilling onto the gas station asphalt, and running down into the twenty-foot-long ditch.

The workers were, of course, astounded, as the trench they were digging filled with soap suds. They were speechless, incredulous, and immobilized by astonishment! Needless to say, we were out of there and back on the highway like a flash, without looking back.

After a lovely visit with Alyce and Ralph, Dave's awe-inspiring parents, we continued on, and two days later, we finally rolled into La Crescenta, the suburb of Los Angeles in which my parents lived. They were overjoyed that we were home and safe. My dad barbequed chuck steaks, as usual, and we shared our extraordinary trip with them, as we ate my mom's, loved by all, potato salad and gazed at the beauty of the San Gabriel Mountains. It was good to be home.

Then Dave broke the relaxing ambiance by stating, "We have to return the car to its owner. I said we'd have it back by tonight."

I jumped up, told my mom we'd be back later for her signature chocolate cake, got the keys from my dad so I could follow Dave in Dad's car, and we took off.

The address of the Cadillac's owner was on Laurel Canyon Boulevard. (This canyon has a lot of history connected to it, with movie stars and rock stars loving the privacy, the woodsy, away-from-the-world aura, and yet the easy access to Hollywood at the end of the canyon.)

As Dave drove the Coupe deVille and I drove behind him down the curvy canyon, full of very expensive houses, set way back from the road among the overhanging trees, I thought to myself, *Yes, the Cadillac belongs in this setting.*

We finally found the address, drove slowly up the long driveway, and parked among several other expensive-looking cars in the parking area. The home was huge and very hidden from the road, as many in the canyon were, so it crossed my mind that a famous person might live there.

The door opened before we could ring the bell, and we were ushered into a large room, occupied by five men who didn't look famous at all. The word I would use is "infamous." I'm not exaggerating in the least when I say they looked as if Central Casting had chosen them and dressed them to look like actors in a Mafia movie. Even I, being much less savvy than Dave, knew we were in trouble!

The man who had let us in quickly locked the door behind us, which didn't help our feeling of danger. We were told to sit down, and then we were questioned (or should I say, "interrogated").

The men sat in a semicircle around us and shot questions at us, like:

"How long did it take you to get from New York City to Los Angeles? Did you stop in any motels along the way?"

We answered that it had taken us four days, and we only stopped once, and that was to sleep at Dave's parents' house. They kept asking if we were sure we hadn't stopped anywhere and if anyone had stopped us, like the police. We assured them we had not stopped and stayed in any motels, and no one, including the police, had stopped us.

The questions kept coming up over and over again, however:

"Did you ever open the trunk? Did you ever have a flat tire? Are you sure you never opened the trunk for any reason?"

After both of us had promised, repeatedly, that we had not opened or looked in the trunk, the men were finally quiet, but they kept looking at each other as if they were trying to decide if they believed us and, more frighteningly, what they were going to do with us. That's when I knew we were in serious trouble, because these were obviously seriously bad men! (I'm sure Dave had realized this the minute we walked into that room.)

I began silently praying. I knew Dave was too. I kept saying over and over to the Lord, "Jesus, please protect us! Please save us!"

Dave, being Dave and always knowing what to do, broke the silence with, "And we need to be paid for the gas we used. That baby drank gas like there was a hole in the tank, and we're out $435."

The men were stunned by Dave's audacity; thankfully, it altered the mood in the room! The men glanced at each other, and the obvious leader stood up, taking a wad of bills out of his wallet.

"Okay, here's your money," he said. "Now get out of here."

We were out the door, in my dad's car, and moving down the driveway with lightning speed, and never looked back!

I could hardly breathe, and when we turned onto Laurel Canyon Boulevard, I started shaking: a delayed reaction.

"How did you ever think of asking them for money when they were surely deciding how they were going to dispose of us?" I whispered.

"I think God gave me the idea and the words," Dave answered quietly.

"Thank the Lord, it worked. I can't believe we got out of there alive. That was such a close call!" I stammered.

Yes, that was such a close call. Way too close, but another time, another example of how Jesus had answered our parents' prayers and our prayers for safety on our trip.

In July, He had spared us from being in the Skopje earthquake, and now, He had saved us from the evil schemes of dangerous men.

As we drove back to La Crescenta to enjoy my mom's chocolate cake, we were so grateful to God, so very, very grateful for being alive. Thank You, Lord.

"Yes, though I walk through the valley of
the shadow of death, I will fear no evil; for
You are with me." (Psalm 23:4a NKJV)

"Though I walk in the midst of trouble, you preserve my
life. You stretch out your hand against the anger of my foes;
with your right hand, you save me." (Psalm 138:7 NIV)

"Cast your cares on the LORD and he will sustain you; he
will never let the righteous be shaken." (Psalm 55:22 NIV)

"The LORD gives strength to his people; the LORD
blesses his people with peace." (Psalm 29:11 NIV)

CHAPTER 9
Angels Came Down

If you have any questions about the reality of Jesus, His angels, or heaven, I pray your doubts will be allayed by reading this chapter.

I'm sure many people feel this way: My dad was the most wonderful father anyone could ask for: loving, forgiving, patient, fun, energetic, creative, and close to the Lord since his childhood. What a role model for the younger men in our family and in our community. Best of all, he was a daily, earthly father example to my brother Tom and me of our heavenly Father's love for us. He always had our best interests at heart and wanted us to be lovingly cared for and happy. We were so blessed.

In addition to Dad's strong faith and character was his strong health. He was never ill and had no injuries (except a bad knee, incurred sliding into home plate while playing baseball for our church), and his male relatives lived into their high nineties. Therefore, it was a devastating shock to the whole family when my dad died suddenly of a heart attack at eighty-four.

In reality, my father's death shouldn't have been as much of a shock to the family as it was, because there was a foreshadowing of heart problems five years earlier. Dad had finally had surgery to repair the knee he'd injured all those years ago, playing baseball on our church's team. A blood clot had broken loose during the operation, gone to Dad's heart, and almost killed him. He miraculously recovered and resumed an active life, but his heart was never quite the same. Because we were all aware of that, Dad's death shouldn't have been such a traumatic, emotional jolt for us. Yet, it was ... and a tremendous loss.

Thirteen years after my dad's passing away, my mom (nicknamed Gigi by her grandchildren) was still going strong at ninety-four, living contentedly in a Covenant Church retirement village near San Diego. We visited her often, driving from Los Angeles for the day, or staying with our son and his family for the weekend, so we could spend time with them and with my mom.

One weekend in particular is never to be forgotten: It began as many others had. Dave and I drove down, picked up my mom, and met our son, his wife, and our two grandsons at a restaurant for good food, good conversation, and most importantly, a good time of being together.

My mom looked wonderful. She was dressed in a beautiful blue pantsuit and walked with her usual purposeful stride, not letting the walker she used slow her down for a minute. Our Marie Fern Ohlund Carlson (called Gigi) was on a roll!

A presidential election was upcoming, and like always, Mom was extremely knowledgeable about candidates, issues, and projections. She had, as long as I could remember, been an ardent follower of politics and current events, both national and international. Now, at almost ninety-five, she was no different. As a result of this, our dinnertime that night was intellectual, interesting, and also great fun, as Mom talked politics and asked the boys (her great-grandsons) about their sports and school, and they told jokes that made us all laugh.

When we returned Mom to Mt. Miguel Retirement Village after dinner, Dave and I stayed and talked with her awhile, as we usually did, relaxing, sharing, and just enjoying being together.

My mom, bless her heart, had the most amazingly optimistic spirit. Several people have told me that just speaking with her once changed their lives. She had been through many tough challenges in her life, but her faith in Jesus, and the intentional decisions that grew out of that faith, set the path for each of her days. The intentional decision she lived by was this, in her words: "Every morning, I have a decision to make, a choice. Am I going to thank Jesus for this new day and live it to the full, no matter what my circumstances, or am I going to focus on myself and my problems. I choose to thank Jesus and be grateful and positive."

That's how my mother lived her life, which is why I was surprised that night, as we talked and shared, how pensive she seemed, a bit down.

Since that was so unlike her, I finally asked, "Mom, is something wrong? You were having such a great time in the restaurant, but now you seem almost teary."

She took a breath and said softly, "I'm really missing your dad. He's been gone thirteen years now, and though I always miss him, it's worse right now because it's almost Valentine's Day. That's a hard day when you're missing the one you'd loved as long as I loved your dad." (They'd been childhood sweethearts and were married for fifty-seven years.)

Mom didn't usually share verbally on this deep level; none of us did. As Scandinavians, we feel strongly, love deeply, care immensely, and outwardly share our emotions haltingly. That night, though, was different. My mom and Dave and I all grew misty-eyed as we shared memories of my dad together.

Then, astoundingly, something happened that touches me to my core any time I think of it. My mom began talking about the night my dad died, in a way she never had before. We knew that my dad had gotten into bed, and Mom was about to follow when she heard him cough; she ran to see if he was all right and found he was gone. My dad had died instantly. This we all knew, but none in the family had ever heard what my mom then shared with Dave and me, now thirteen years later. (I want to add that my mother was not an exaggerator, an embellisher, or an emotional storyteller; therefore, we knew what she was telling us was absolutely accurate.) Here, in her own words, is what she recounted to us that night, a few days before Valentine's Day:

"Daddy had just gotten into bed, and I had just finished brushing my teeth. I heard him cough and went to see if he was okay. The sight I saw I'll never forget! The room was filled with angels, Jesus had Daddy in His arms, and they took him up."

At first, Dave and I were speechless. Then I cried, "Mom, why didn't you ever tell us about this before? It's amazing, a miracle that the Lord let you see. You saw Jesus come to carry Dad to heaven? Why didn't you tell us?"

She hesitated and said softly, "It was such a gift from the Lord, to let me see Him take Daddy. I kept it inside, close to my heart, as a comfort because I have missed Daddy so much. But I wanted to share this with you tonight."

Four days later, on Valentine's Day, Dave and I understood why the Holy Spirit had prompted Mom to tell us of the miraculous way Jesus had come to take Daddy to be with Him. For, on Valentine's Day, the Lord also took my mom to heaven. She came down with a cold that morning but assured me when I spoke to her during my daily call that it was just a cold, and she would be fine. Hours later, she could not breathe, and she passed away, peacefully, in an ambulance.

I have thanked God many, many times that we stayed to talk with my mom after the family dinner and that she told us she had seen angels and had seen Jesus carry Dad in His arms. She shared that miracle with us just days before she died, and if she hadn't, we would never have known.

Other wonderful miracles have happened to members of our family, but this one needs to be remembered, recounted, and put down in written words. I am grateful God has enabled me to do so, and I'm very, very grateful I had my precious mother with me all those years, and that our children and grandchildren also deeply loved Gigi. Once again, thank You, Lord.

"Are not all angels ministering spirits sent to serve those who will inherit salvation?" (Hebrews 1:14 NIV)

(Jesus is speaking.)

"Do not let your hearts be troubled. You believe in God; believe also in me. My Father's house has many rooms; if that were not so, would I have told you that I'm going there to prepare a place for you? And if I go and prepare a place for you, I will come back and take you to be with me that you also may be where I am." (John 14:1–3 NIV)

"But blessed is the one who trust in the LORD, whose confidence is in him." (Jeremiah 17:7 NIV)

"You [Lord] will keep him in perfect peace, whose mind is stayed on You, because he trusts in You." (Isaiah 26:3 NKJV)

CHAPTER 10

You Never Know
Who's Listening

This chapter is about Hanson family miracles in Siberia. Yes, Siberia. Hang on, and you'll see why.

I've already shared several stories about Dave's dad (Grandpa Hanson to our children, and Great-Grandpa Ralph to our grandchildren). He was an awe-inspiring man, full of faith and fearlessness, as he pursued what God told him to do.

As I related earlier, Dave's dad and mom were missionaries in small Eskimo villages on the Seward Peninsula, in northern Alaska. The village in which they built a home and church, White Mountain, and the other hamlets where they concentrated their ministries were diminutive then and remain so to this day.

In fact, some of those towns have very few residents during the winter months now and are only populated in the summer, with most going to live in Nome for the duration of Alaska's fierce winters. However, when Dave's folks were missionaries there, telling Eskimos that Jesus was real and loved them, the villages were the heart of their ministry.

Even today, the stories of Whirlwind Hanson still remain, and Ralph is remembered and revered, for he brought the gospel message to those hamlets and Nome as well.

As I stated in another chapter, Dave's parents had to leave Alaska when Dave was a child, due to his mom's ill health, and his dad subsequently was elected the Executive Secretary of World Missions for the Evangelical Covenant Church of America. (This meant he was in charge of all the missionaries and mission outreach, and needed to move to Chicago, where the Covenant denomination was headquartered. Hence, Dave grew up in the same church as I, in Chicago, and that is where we met as children. Thank You, Lord.)

The heart of this matter is, though, that in spite of the fact that Dave's father, in his new position, was instrumental in establishing new mission outreaches in Mexico, Ecuador, Taiwan, Japan, and Indonesia, as well as expanding the health and education work in the Republic of Congo, Ralph Hanson's heart was still in Alaska. That place and those people were his first love as a missionary and always would be.

Therefore, along with all the other projects he inspired and helped to carry out while he was Secretary of World Missions, Ralph was the guiding light for the landmark building and opening of KICY, a radio station in Nome, Alaska. And, the opening of that radio station is how this book's chapter relates to Siberia.

For years, Dad had dreamed of a Christian radio station in northern Alaska that would broadcast programs throughout Alaska and also into the eastern part of Russia's Soviet Union, called Siberia. When KICY opened, our country was in the midst of a Cold War with Russia, and their leaders were trying to stamp out Christian influences in the Soviet Union. A radio station that could beam programs behind Russia's Iron Curtain, where Christianity was not allowed, had long been a prayer of Ralph Hanson.

A bit of history: In the early 1920s, the Soviet Union was established in Russia and was later expanded in the surrounding countries that were overtaken by Russia. Since the Communist ideology is atheistic, one of the major goals of the Soviet leaders was to eliminate religion and replace it with atheism. For this reason, they systematically closed churches, persecuted Christians, and mandated that atheism be taught in all schools.)

With the above facts in mind, you can see why Dave's dad, and countless others, would want to beam Christian programs into Siberia, also called the Russian Far East. Not only could these broadcasts be a support to any Christians in Siberia who'd gone "underground" and were meeting secretly in homes, but young people who had grown up being taught only atheism in their schools might possibly hear the good news about Jesus Christ.

Consequently, on Easter Sunday, 1960, KICY went on the air, sending weather reports, music, Bible readings, and messages sharing the love of Jesus throughout Alaska and into Eastern Russia. On staff were various broadcasters, who among them spoke Eskimo dialects, Russian, and English. The programs were immediately well received and praised by those hearing KICY's offerings in Alaska.

Christians and non-Christians alike greatly appreciated the weather reports, which were crucial to survival in the often formidable and always changeable weather. Believers, of course, were thrilled by the Bible passages and uplifting devotional messages, and many others also reported that they had become believers in Jesus through listening to KICY.

Yet the one thing that was never reported was whether or not Russian authorities were blocking KICY's transmissions into Siberia; no one knew whether anyone there was listening to the programs. Thus, for years (decades, actually), no one knew whether KICY was being heard in the Russian Far East or having any effect there at all.

Then, remarkably, in the late 1980s, the Soviet Union began to collapse, and on Christmas Day, 1991, the Soviet flag flew over the Communist headquarters in Moscow for the last time. It was replaced by the Russian flag, because the country of Russia remained intact, but the many surrounding countries that had been controlled by Russia's terrifying iron fist for decades were now free and becoming independent once again. It was a glorious day for them and the world!

With the dissolution of the Soviet Union also came a lessening of some harsh controls and severe restrictions in the farther reaches of Russia, especially the Russian Far East (Siberia). Some slight cracks in the Iron Curtain started appearing, bringing about totally unexpected, serendipitous occurrences. One of these astounding developments was a phone call to KICY from a government official in Provideniya, Siberia, asking to speak to someone who spoke Russian.

Fortunately, the station manager did, as well as several others, and he quickly came to the phone. (Remember, there had been no contact, ever, between KICY and Siberia since the radio station's opening, more than three decades earlier. Even more astounding than the call, however, was what the Russian official said:

"I am the head of the Provideniya Cultural Department, and I want you to know that we in Provideniya have been listening to your broadcasts since you began, and we greatly appreciate the weather reports. We rely on them. And, we enjoy the classical music, much of which is by our own Russian composers."

The KICY station manager was beyond astounded at the conversation and was being gracious in his replies, when suddenly, as the Russian official continued, the truly miraculous happened:

"There's one more thing," the Russian stated, and then he paused. "Many of us have also listened to your religious programs, and we were wondering if you could bring us some Bibles."

Some Bibles? The KICY manager, shocked, thought to himself, *Is this real or some kind of not-so-funny joke?*

"As you know," the Russian went on, "Provideniya is just a few hundred miles from Nome, only separated by the Bering Strait. It would be greatly appreciated if we could set a date and time for your visit."

The station manager was silent for a moment as he caught his breath, heart pounding and mind whirling with these private thoughts: *Yes! We've been separated all these years by your government's mandates, not by miles. But now things must be changing. This is almost unbelievable. Astonishing. People in Provideniya have been listening for decades, and we haven't known. And now they want Bibles. How absolutely great is the Lord! What a miracle!"*

Recovering some composure, the manager finally answered, "I'm sure we can visit and bring Bibles. It will be wonderful to meet you. Please give me your name and phone number, and I'll arrange our trip to Provideniya as soon as possible."

Hence, that heaven-sent phone call began a series of events that touched many hearts.

Alyce, Dave's mom, had passed away several years earlier, and Dave's dad had married Lillian (Lil), whom we all adored. (Alyce and Ralph and Lil and her husband, Ernie, had been best friends through the years, and when both Ralph and Lil had lost their beloved spouses to death, they consoled each other in their grief, and later fell in love and married: a beautiful story.)

Dad was now in his eighties, and he and Lil were living in a lovely Covenant retirement complex on Mercer Island, Washington, when Dad received the call from KICY, Nome.

"Ralph," he began, "this is the station manager at KICY with some extraordinary news and a question for you." Dave's father was always thrilled to hear from Alaska and had visited many times through the years, as well as spear-heading and helping with numerous new projects and outreaches there. His heart had remained in those villages and with the Eskimos he so loved.

"It's so good to hear from you," Ralph answered. "What's the extraordinary news and question?"

The KICY manager told about the call from Siberia and related his conversation with the Russian government official, word for word. Even Dave's dad, who was never surprised by miracles (in fact, he counted on them), was shocked by the news.

"Oh, that's marvelous," he said. "Wonderful! They've been listening all these years? And they want Bibles? Hallelujah is all I can say. Hallelujah! When are you bringing them?"

"Well, that's where the question comes in. I called Covenant headquarters in Chicago, spoke with several in different positions there, and told them of this absolutely momentous and completely unexpected request. They, too, were shocked and thrilled, and said of course they would get a large supply of Bibles in the Russian language for us to bring. Next, the president of Covenant came on the line and said, 'You know, there's someone who was the guiding light for the building of KICY and one who wanted the programs to be broadcast in Russian, as well as in English and in Eskimo dialect. That person is Ralph Hanson. He should lead our delegation to Provideniya.'

"So, Ralph, are you willing and able to go?"

God is so gracious! Dave's parents had gone to Alaska in the 1930's, bringing Bibles and sharing the good news of Jesus's love,; and now, sixty-some years later, the Lord was giving Dad the gift of being able to go to Russia, again bringing Bibles and sharing Jesus's love. God had let Dave's dad, through the years, see the results of seeds sown in Alaska: ---people believing in Christ and, churches, orphanages, and schools being built. Now, the Lord was letting Dad see the results of seeds being sown for many decades in Siberia: ---people longing for Bibles and the good news of the gospel.

Therefore, several weeks later, Dave's extraordinary father (in his late eighties) and Lil led a delegation of Covenant leaders and KICY employees to Provideniya, Siberia, bringing Bibles and God's love. Hallelujah! Hallelujah, indeed! What a wonderful Lord.

EPILOGUE

Fact is always so much more amazing than fiction could ever be, and this epilogue, regarding Dad and Lil's trip to Siberia, certainly upholds that truism. You'll hardly be able to believe what I'm going to share.

Dad and Lil had a cozy cabin in the Santa Cruz Mountains of Northern California, built by Lil's grandfather and remodeled, much later, by Dad and Lil. It was on the grounds of a Covenant Church campground, lush with trees, hills, and much-loved family cabins: a place Dave and I always looked forward to visiting with great anticipation.

Okay, here's the unbelievable part: A few months after Dad and Lil had led the delegation to Siberia, they were enjoying a spectacular summer day at their cabin in Mission Springs, when there came a knock at the door.

Answering without hesitation, because many friends visited each day for a cup of coffee and Swedish coffee cake, Lil swung wide the door with a welcoming smile.

To her utter amazement, though, it was not a friend coming by for coffee, but several Russian officials they had met when they brought Bibles to Siberia.

What are they doing on our doorstep? thought a very shocked Lil. *How did they get here, and however in the world did they find us?*

The answers to the first two questions soon became apparent: The Russians flew from Provideniya, Siberia, to Nome, Alaska; from Nome to Seattle; and from Seattle to San Jose, California, subsequently driving down to the Mission Springs campground in Scotts Valley.

The "why" they were there was also soon explained: They were on a mission. How they had found Dave's dad and Lil in their cabin, ten miles north of Santa Cruz, nestled in the mountains, is still a mystery. (I guess Russians officials can find out most things they want to know, if they try.)

The reason this delegation of officials was there, having Swedish coffee with Dad and Lil, is to me, almost beyond belief. They were there because they had been so impressed with Dave's father in Siberia that the city's officials met and decided Dad should be the cultural emissary for Provideniya. He would go back and forth between Russian Siberia and the United States as a goodwill ambassador, bringing groups of people from each country to encounter, appreciate, and enjoy the culture of both countries. What? Wow! You're kidding! A great idea, but Dad was almost ninety, and Lil wasn't that far behind.

Dad and Lil were speechless, especially Lil. Dad never seemed to be shocked by incredible adventures that came his way. In fact, we had never known him to turn down an adventure, even a life-threatening one, because he always believed they were from the Lord and part of the mission that God had for him. So Dad was excited and raring to go on this next adventure, to Siberia.

Lil being speechless and Dad immediately ready to be an ambassador for Provideniya was typical on both counts. Lil, since they'd been married, had always been a bit shocked when Ralph had told her of their next trip to visit Covenant mission stations. This is what he had done when he was Executive Secretary of World Missions and continued to do, at times, long after retirement.

He and Lil had been to Alaska several times, to South America, and on a lengthy trip to Asian countries together, visiting with missionaries and giving them encouragement. Lil was very supportive and joined Dad on his trips and adventures with unusual grace. Even so, this time was different.

Sensing Lil's reticence and reluctance to another out-of-the-country adventure, Ralph, instead of saying his usual, yes, said they would pray about the enticing offer and call the head official in a few days with their answer.

Common sense (and "Lil's sense") prevailed, for though Dave's father was fit, his health was not what it had been in earlier days, and he was near ninety.

Therefore, after much prayer together and communication about the pros and cons, Dad, though he was very honored by the offer of this high position, declined graciously. Provideniya would have to find a different cultural ambassador.

As I stated at the beginning of this epilogue, here was another almost-unbelievable episode in the life of Ralph Hanson, Dave's exceptional, loving dad and my exceptional, loving father-in-law.

POSTSCRIPT

There's also a postscript to this chapter, and surprisingly, it's about my parents, for my mom and dad had a heart for Alaska too. Several years after they had both retired, Dave and Marie Carlson (my parents) volunteered to be short-term missionaries in Nome, Alaska. They were gladly accepted by leaders of the Evangelical Covenant Church, and they spent several exciting, memorable months working in Nome.

My mom, a fantastic, natural-born cook, made breakfast, lunch, dinner, homemade bread, and desserts for all the workers at KICY, the Covenant radio station. (This sounds terrifying to me.) My dad, who could build or fix anything, was the handyman: building, creating, and repairing whatever needed attention at the radio station, church, and Covenant workers' homes. My parents labored from early morning to late at night, loving their assignments and all those with whom they were working.

Thus, you can see that Jesus has put Alaska in the heart of Dave's family and mine. In fact, one of our nephews was an announcer and program presenter at KICY after college, and there may be more Hansons serving in Nome in coming years. We do not know the future, but thankfully, we know the Lord does. Amen.

"Let us not become weary in doing good, for at the proper time we will reap a harvest if we do not give up." (Galatians 6:9 NIV)

"So then faith comes by hearing, and hearing by the word of God." (Romans 10:17 NKJV)

(Jesus is speaking.)

"And this gospel of the kingdom will be preached in all the world as a witness to all the nations." (Matthew 24:14a NKJV)

"Your word is a lamp for my feet, a light on my path." (Psalm 119:105 NIV)

"This is what the Sovereign LORD says: 'those who hope in me will not be disappointed.'" (Isaiah 49: 22a, 23b NIV)

(The Lord is speaking.)

"For as the rain comes down, and the snow from heaven, and do not return there, but water the earth, and make it bring forth and bud, that it may give seed to the sower and bread to the eater, so shall My word be that goes forth from My mouth; it shall not return to Me void, but it shall accomplish what I please, and it shall prosper in the thing for which I sent it." (Isaiah 55:10, 11 NKJV)

"This is good, and pleases God our Savior, who wants all people to be saved and to come to a knowledge of the truth." (1 Timothy 2:3, 4 NIV)

CHAPTER 11
To Fly Like an Eagle

Have you ever had God send an eagle into your midst to encourage you? Sound crazy? Well, it was crazy, and utterly breath-taking.

In my first book, *Extraordinary Miracles for an Ordinary Family*, I detailed how my family had become involved in Creation Care. I told how our two oldest sons had hiked the entire Pacific Crest Trail from Mexico to Canada and discovered clear-cuts (no standing trees) in national forests all the way from mid-California to the end of the trail in Canada.

These shocking sights were the impetus for our sons to seek out answers to the questions: Who is allowing our country's national forests to be devastatingly logged by multinational corporations at US taxpayer expense, and why is this destruction being allowed?

These questions ultimately led one of our sons to found a forest protection organization, the John Muir Project (JMP), and our whole family helped found the Religious Campaign for Forest Conservation (RCFC). We are all still active in striving to protect our national forests and all of God's precious creation.

After the inception of JMP and RCFC, many years ago now, our daughter, Beth, and I felt we needed to go to Washington DC to speak with lawmakers about the commercial logging and clear-cutting of national forests, and publicize the fact that taxpayer money was used to subsidize the multinational companies doing the logging. We also wanted to bring material with us that would show God's love for His creation and His mandates in the Bible about caring for creation.

Regarding this, Beth and I somehow came up with the idea for a perpetual calendar, with each day of the year having a Bible verse or quotation from a revered Christian, addressing the need to protect God's creation.

I shared our plans to go to DC with our dear friend, Fred Krueger, who was director of the newly founded RCFC.

He quickly replied, "We should all go. I'll put this out to other RCFC members, and we'll see who can join us. This will take much prayer and organization, but we need to do this. We need to tell Congress that the Lord loves His forests and the creatures who desperately need those forests to survive. We'll print handouts that show intact, old-growth forests and that also show what forests look like when they've been clear-cut and destroyed. Let's highlight the Bible verses we stand upon that call for Creation Care. We're going to DC!"

Thus began the first RCFC Washington Week, in 1999, and members of the group have gone every year since. (Over the years, the name has changed from RCFC to NRCCC, the National Religious Coalition on Creation Care, but our message is the same: The Lord wants us to protect His creation and the people and creatures therein.)

Miracles occur every time we bring God's message to DC, but the ones that happened during the first RCFC visit have a special place in my memory and heart. We were a little band of believers from all over the country, and we began that year, as we always do, with a prayer breakfast. That year, our breakfast was at the Willard Hotel, in the Round Robin Room. It was a time of praying, singing, sharing, fellowship, and bonding with sisters and brothers from around the nation.

As our special prayer breakfast came to a close, we exited out onto Pennsylvania Avenue, intending to walk the one and a half miles to Capitol Hill and the Congressional office buildings. However, as we left the hotel, we noticed limousines pulling up to another part of the Willard and dignitaries being ushered into the building. Fred asked one of the limousine drivers what his passenger was attending, and the answer was, "There's a convention of all the US governors going on in there."

All the governors? We stopped immediately, and Tom, from Wisconsin, proposed, "One of us should go in to see if it's possible to speak to the governors."

We quickly appointed Tom, but before he went in, we formed a prayer circle on the sidewalk to pray for him and ask that the Lord would open doors, minds, and hearts inside. Holding hands and praying fervently, we hardly noticed at first that something truly amazing had happened:

While we were praying, a little sparrow had appeared and landed right in our midst, in the middle of our prayer circle, and stayed there, not moving. We continued to pray, and the sparrow stayed. We ended by singing the Doxology, and still the sparrow stayed. Not until we broke apart and Tom went into the Willard did the little bird fly away. We all commented on how unusual it was that it had flown into the midst of us and stayed. (We didn't realize till later how unusual it really was.)

I can't say that the governors welcomed Tom and his message with open arms, but he did have the chance to speak with several and share what we felt God was leading us to do and why. They were interested in the fact that we were coming from a faith-based position, backed up by Bible verses and passages. Believing the Lord was answering our prayers, we continued our walk toward Capitol Hill.

As our group neared the Capitol building, its dome gleaming in sunlight, Fred suggested we stop on the lawn, below the many great stairs leading up to the Capitol's entrance, and pray again before visiting lawmakers in the Congressional office buildings nearby. Gladly, we formed another circle and began to pray. This time, something even more astounding and amazing happened than the last time:

This time, it was an eagle! An enormous, beautiful, glorious bald eagle landed in our midst. Again, right in the middle of our prayer circle, and it stayed. Yes, and stayed. We were all so shocked that we faltered and, understandably, stopped praying.

Then, one of us said, "The Lord has given us signs today that He is with us. This eagle is another miraculous sign. Let's pray a while longer."

And we did, with the magnificent bald eagle, one of God's most wondrous creatures, listening and staying. Staying in our midst.

Just as we were finishing praying, though, a frantic voice came nearer, shouting, "Has anyone seen my eagle? He was supposed to soar over the Capitol when I released him and then return to my arm, as he always does. We were way up on the Capitol veranda, and he soared but then flew down here, to the back lawn. Have you seen him? I'm desperate."

As we dropped hands and broke the circle, our feathered guest flew over to his extremely worried friend.

"Oh, thank God I've found him," he cried. "He's never done that before, not coming back, I mean. I don't know what got into him."

The relieved man started to calm down, and we began explaining who we were, why we were in DC, and why we were praying.

"That's very interesting," he replied. "Challenger here and I," he nodded toward the huge eagle resting on his arm, "are in DC for a similar reason. He travels around the country, under the care of the American Eagle Foundation, as an advocate for wildlife protection. Challenger has done free-flying appearances across the nation at such events as the World Series, bowl games, the opening ceremony at the Olympics in Atlanta, and at the White House and US Capitol. Most importantly, he's been key in getting grants from Congress to help prevent species from becoming endangered or extinct. That's why we're here this week: to remind Congress that once an animal becomes endangered, it takes much more work and money to save them from extinction than to protect them in the first place."

Heartily agreeing that we were on the same team as Challenger, we shared that while we wanted Congress to protect national forests because they purify the air we all breathe and provide places of beauty and recreation, we were also striving to end the destruction of the habitat wildlife needs for their very survival.

It was then time for us to go to our meetings and Challenger to continuing preparing for his next event, but as we parted, his friend mused, "You had a very important eagle praying with you today."

"Yes," we agreed. "We'll never forget this." And we never have.

When Beth and I were in our room later that night, I began reflecting on the various events of the day, the numerous parts, and slowly the pieces fit together. I saw, once again, how personal is our God, how He lovingly shows us what He wants us to do and that He is with us.

First, we just happened to have our prayer breakfast in the Round Robin Room. Next, a sparrow just happened to join our prayer circle on the sidewalk. And finally, a bald eagle, named Challenger, just happened to join our prayer time at the Capitol.

You can make of all this what you like, but I believe the Lord was telling us, "I love my creatures, my forests, my creation. Keep on working, my children. I'm with you."

Amen.

"Wail, you juniper, for the cedar has fallen; the stately
trees are ruined! Wail, oaks of Bashan; the dense
forest has been cut down!" (Zechariah 11:2 NIV)

"The trees of the LORD are well watered, the cedars
of Lebanon that he planted. There the birds make their
nests; the stork has its home in the junipers. The high
mountains belong to the wild goats; the crags are a refuge
for the hyrax [rock badger]." (Psalm 104:16–18 NIV)

"Then the LORD said to Noah, … 'You shall take with you
seven each of every clean animal, a male and his female; two
each of animals that are unclean, a male and his female; also
seven each of birds of the air, male and female, to keep the
species alive on the face of all the earth.'" (Genesis 7:1a–3)

"But those who hope in the LORD will renew
their strength. They will soar on wings like
eagles; they will run and not grow weary, they
will walk and not be faint." (Isaiah 40:31 NIV)

(The Lord is speaking.)

"You have seen what I did to the Egyptians, and
how I bore you on eagles' wings and brought
you to Myself." (Exodus 19:4 NKJV)

"He [God] shall cover you with His feathers, and
under His wings you shall take refuge; His truth shall
be your shield and buckler." (Psalm 91:4 NKJV)

"The earth is the LORD's, and everything in it, the
world, and all who live in it." (Psalm 24:1 NIV)

CHAPTER 12
Jesus Was There

If you want to be confident of the fact that Jesus is real and that He is with you, read this chapter and be assured.

I deeply love my cousin Chris. She and her younger brother, Rick, and my younger brother Tom and I were raised as though we were all brothers and sisters, not cousins, and we love each other as such.

Our mothers, Marie and Bee, were sisters who also deeply loved each other. Auntie Bee had lived with us for a while in Chicago, and then when she married Uncle Len and moved to California, my parents and Tom and I followed suit and moved to California too, living with Auntie Bee and Uncle Len until we had a home of our own. (My maternal grandparents had followed Bee to California a year earlier, so we were all together again, this time in La Crescenta, in the Golden Gate State.)

I was years older than Chris, but the age difference didn't keep us from understanding each other, being close, and having a family history bond, learned from our mothers, that was special to us. As I said, we were sisters.

That's why her phone call to me, while I was buying gift wrap in Rite Aid drugstore, was tremendously shattering.

As I held a package of birthday wrapping paper in my hand, I heard my cell phone ring and saw it was Chris.

"Hi, Chris! How are you?" I asked, heading for the checkout counter.

"Not good," she whispered.

And then, because she followed with words I was sure I'd heard incorrectly, I hurriedly answered, "I can't hear well, so I'm going out into the parking lot." After I went outside, I asked Chris to repeat what I was positive I'd not heard clearly.

"I'm in the hospital," she began, "and the doctor just told me I only have a few months to live. I was having trouble breathing, so I took a taxi to get here. I've had tests, and the doctor just told me the results."

Stunned and in utter disbelief, I cried, "Chris, this can't be true! They've made a terrible mistake! The tests can't possibly be right. I'll get Dave, and we'll be there in minutes!"

We were there in minutes, and we met Rick and his wife, Joni, in the hospital hallway.

Falling into each other's arms, Joni and I sobbed and repeated, "This can't be true. This can't be true." Then the four of us prayed and walked together into Chris's room.

As always, in spite of the doctor's terrifying pronouncement, Chris was her usual positive, cheerful self. (How could she be? I couldn't imagine.) She then reiterated to all of us what had been told to her. The diagnosis was inoperable, advanced lung cancer.

None of us could believe, could internalize, could accept that Chris was dying and, especially, that there was nothing the doctors could do.

As we began discussing ("there must be something they can do"), a young, soft-spoken, compassionate, yet forceful doctor appeared, and without much introduction, she stated, "We're so sorry, very sorry, but our tests have shown that Chris has inoperable, advanced cancer in both lungs. She most likely has one or two months to live."

At first there was silence in the room, and then the four of us began asking questions:

"Are you sure? Isn't there anything you can try? How do you know you're correct?"

The doctor was patient but unchanging with her replies. This was their diagnosis. This was their prognosis. There was no hope.

Joni and I were teary and trying not to break down again. Rick and Dave were grim faced with clenched jaws. And Chris? Chris was stoic and almost peaceful, as though she had already moved toward acceptance.

We stayed and prayed together in the hospital room, and then Joni and I left for a few minutes to call family, friends, and prayer groups, asking that they all pray for Chris. I was asking for prayers for miraculous healing, in which we believe.

That night, when we had returned home, my dear friend Ann texted, "I'm praying for Chris! And I had this thought ... Ask her what she wants us to pray for."

I texted back that I would, and the next day, when we went again to the hospital, I asked Chris that very question: "What do you want us to pray for," and was surprised and deeply touched by her answer.

She looked at me, not with tears, not with anger or self-pity, but with earnestness and said, "Please pray I go up to heaven quickly and easily, for Joni, Rick, and Alyssa's sake." (Alyssa is Joni and Rick's daughter, treasured by Chris and all of us.)

Simple words, "Pray I go up quickly and easily for their sake," yet holding so much meaning, for Joni and Rick were at home, making ready the room they would be bringing Chris to the next day, where they would lovingly care for her during her last days on earth.

I promised Chris I would pray that prayer and that we all would be praying that prayer for her. With certainty, the Lord answered, as He always does.

About a month later, Chris and Joni and I had been watching old movies on TV all day, and it was time to get Chris settled in bed for the night. Since leaving the hospital, Chris's breathing had been somewhat labored, but oxygen had helped, and miraculously, she'd had no pain. No pain; what a miracle. And that night, as we helped her into bed, she was the same: No pain, but shallow, difficult breathing, and she was very weak.

I am not at all good with anything medical, and I was feeling quite weak myself that night at the sight of Chris, just clinging to life. After Joni and I prayed for her at her bedside, Chris whispered, "Amen," and then I saw the most overwhelming sight, more overwhelming than I can put down in words. I saw a white light and then a shining figure on the other side of the bed, standing by Chris's head. The person was bright and yet calming and so radiant. So radiant. I knew with an absolute assurance that it was Jesus. A peace came over me I've never felt before or since. Jesus was there. Jesus was there with Chris, with us; all was well.

In the comfort of Jesus's presence, I whispered good night to Chris and told her I loved her. She murmured she loved me, and I left, still in a sense of awe and wonder at what I had seen.

Just a few hours later, in the early morning hours, Rick called to say Chris had gone to heaven: great sorrow for us, but great glory for her.

But "sorrow" is only partly true, for Jesus had answered her prayer to go quickly and easily. And He had assured me, and now you, the reader, that He took Chris to be with Himself, to heaven, where there are no tears, just joy, and that is what Chris is experiencing forever: pure joy.

Later when I described to Joni my experience of seeing Jesus at Chris's bedside, she shared with tears in her eyes that the same thing had happened to her when her beloved mother was dying in her arms. Joni had seen Jesus, right with them, ready to take her mother into His arms.

What a compassionate, loving Lord. Not only taking our loved ones to heaven, but letting us know, without a shadow of a doubt, that they are with Him. "Thank You, Lord. Thank You, Lord. Thank You, Lord."

"Surely he [Jesus] took up our pain and bore
our suffering." (Isaiah 53:4a NIV)

"The LORD replied, 'My Presence will go with you,
and I will give you rest.'" (Exodus 33:14 NIV)

"Jesus answered him, 'Truly I tell you, today you
will be with me in paradise.'" (Luke 23:43 NIV)

"We have this hope as an anchor for the soul,
firm and secure." (Hebrews 6:19a NIV)

CHAPTER 13
To Live Another Day, Again

In the last chapter of my previous book, *Extraordinary Miracles for an Ordinary Family*, I told of Dave's near-death experience, explaining that the Lord had let him "live another day" (and, thankfully, many days after that). Little did I know when I penned those words that, terrifyingly, yet miraculously, there would be another near-death experience to be recounted in this book.

The day had started like any other. I was making breakfast, and Dave was getting out of bed and going into the den, where we would eat breakfast while watching the morning news. Then, in a second, everything changed. I'll never forget that morning, not now, not ever! I'll never forget.

It began as usual, as momentous days often do, with Dave watching the news and me making breakfast in the kitchen.

It was the beginning of a normal day, I thought, an uneventful day. How wrong I was.

I brought our trays into the den, intending to eat while we watched our local newscaster give the weather report and tell what had happened in LA overnight.

Handing Dave his tray and sitting down beside him, as I did on any ordinary day, I asked, "Anything interesting on the news this morning?"

He looked at me, was quiet for a moment, and then answered in garbled, unintelligible words. I, of course, thought he was kidding around, but he tried again to answer me, and his words were still completely nonsensical and garbled. Nothing like this had ever happened to either of us before!

I was slightly panicked, but not in full panic yet because Dave has type 2 diabetes, and I thought this might be some strange low-blood-sugar reaction. I grabbed my cellphone and texted my dear cousin, Joni, with the words, "Call me!"

(Joni's husband, my cousin Rick, is a paramedic with the Los Angeles Fire Department; family members often call Rick first when we have a medical question, because he always knows what to do.)

Rick was usually at the fire station, but I knew Joni would get my text, call me, and then call Rick. This is when the first miracle of that tumultuous day occurred. Rick was, providentially, at home. He and Joni were working in the yard, but he had come in to get a glass of water and heard the incoming "beep" on Joni's cell, which was lying on the kitchen counter. He looked down and saw my message: "Call me!"

Knowing that an imperative, short message was not like me, Rick called immediately and said, "Lee, what's wrong?"

When I told him Dave was talking incoherently and couldn't say one intelligible word, Rick stated firmly, "Hang up and call 911, now."

I did, immediately, and then God brought another miracle. Within minutes, I could hear the paramedics' siren coming closer. We have one fire station in South Pasadena, and if they'd been out at another emergency, help would have had to come from an adjacent town, taking longer.

I'll never forget the care, concern, and competence of those wonderful paramedics and firemen. They examined Dave, talked to him, and knew right away that he was in serious trouble. As they tried to calm and comfort me, they helped Dave onto a stretcher and into the ambulance. (He could still walk at that time, but not speak.) The rescuers took off up our hill with sirens blaring, and I was told to follow in my car, which I did.

Before leaving the driveway, however, I first called our daughter. Here's the next miracle: Beth usually can't be reached by phone at work, but on that day, right at that moment, she'd left her office to walk across the campus on an errand.

She answered her cell on the first ring, and I told her, "Dad is on his way to the hospital! Please call your brothers, and Tom and Dolley [my brother and sister-in-law], and the Covenant Group [my prayer group]. Ask them to pray, and then meet me at the hospital. I love you!"

By then, I was crying as I pulled out of the driveway.

Beth called her brothers (David in San Diego, Christopher in Scottsdale, and Thomas in Big Bear) and also Tom and Dolley and the Covenant Group. She then ran to her car for the short drive to the hospital where Dave had been taken.

Meanwhile, Joni and Rick, bless their hearts, had jumped into their car and had arrived at the emergency room entrance just before the ambulance carrying Dave arrived. Having Cousin Rick there was absolutely invaluable because he'd brought people to that emergency room many, many times and knew exactly how things worked and how to help. (He confided later that Dave's right side was paralyzed by the time he was wheeled into the hospital, and he was unconscious. Dave remembers nothing after the first part of the ambulance ride.)

When I pulled up to the hospital, Rick was waiting out in front; he said he would park my car and that I should go right in the main door where doctors were already waiting for me. He wasn't exaggerating that doctors were waiting. I was inundated with people in white coats holding clipboards; some were doctors, and some were other hospital personnel.

I was told that my husband had a blood clot in his brain and they needed my permission to give him a drug that might dissolve the clot. I quickly signed the papers, and the doctors sped off.

The two young women remaining in the room needed me to fill out forms about Dave, which I did; and, it was comforting to me that the young women's names were Beth and Candy, the names of our daughter and our niece. I was praying that was a sign from the Lord.

Shortly after I'd finished filling out the forms for Beth and Candy, Rick came into the room, followed by the doctors I'd seen several minutes before.

One stepped forward and said urgently, "Mrs. Hanson, the medicine did not dissolve the clot in your husband's brain, and I have to do surgery immediately. Otherwise, there's no chance to save him. I need you to sign these papers, and we'll take him to the operating room right now. I also need to tell you that we may lose him, and even if he lives, he may be severely impaired. But if we don't do the surgery, he'll surely die or remain in a vegetative state the rest of his life."

I was too traumatized to even breathe and thought I would faint, but thank the Lord, Rick was there.

He said, "Sign the papers, Lee. Sign the papers. This surgery is Dave's only hope."

I signed the papers, and the doctors literally sprinted out of the room and down the hall.

After they had left, reality started hitting, and I thought I might break down; I couldn't hold it together. Then, however, the Lord reminded me of another miracle that had just taken place:

When the doctor who was going to do the surgery had put out his hand to introduce himself, he had said, "I'm Dr. Constance; I'll be the one operating on your husband."

Dr. Constance? That's my name! Constance Lee Hanson! I took that as a loving sign from Jesus that He was with Dave, with me, with us. I immediately felt a sense of peace in the midst of the terrible storm.

Rick and I were ushered into the room where families waited while loved ones were in the operating room, and when we entered, Joni came rushing over, and Beth ran in at the same time, out of breath, and beyond worried.

We all hugged, and Beth cried, "Where's Dad? Can I see him?"

"He's in surgery," I answered, and I shared what Dr. Constance had told me. As tears began to roll down our faces, Dolley and Tom arrived, and Beth repeated the dire circumstances and terrifying prognosis ahead if the blood clot could not be eliminated.

In one accord, we grabbed each other's hands, formed a prayer circle in the middle of the waiting room, and prayed that Dave would be protected. We asked Jesus to guide the surgeon's hands; enable Dr. Constance to eradicate the blood clot; and, that Dave would be miraculously saved and restored. We begged for this, in the powerful name of Jesus. Then we waited and prayed, waited and prayed, waited and prayed.

During this excruciating time of uncertainty, another small miracle happened! Our son, Thomas, had been trying to get down the mountain from Big Bear, through non-moving traffic, and when finally arriving, had rushed into the emergency room to be told his dad was no longer in the E R, but was now in an operating room on the other side of the hospital!

Seeing Thomas's deep concern, an intern offered to show him the way to the surgery waiting room, where the rest of us were. Here's the small miracle I mentioned, with major results: The intern was a Christian, and as he and Thomas hurried through the labyrinthine halls of the huge hospital, the intern prayed aloud that Jesus would protect Dave's life and heal him. A praying helper. Thank you. Lord.

Then, minutes before Thomas reached us, Dr. Constance appeared in his scrubs and spoke the words I was desperate to hear:

"I was able to remove the clot in his brain. He's alive and conscious, and being taken to ICU."

"Praise God! Thank You, Jesus!" we all kept repeating. What a blessing. What a miraculous answer to prayer. Dave was alive; he was conscious!

I also thanked Dr. Constance profusely, and after listening, he murmured solemnly, "It doesn't always turn out this way."

I thanked him again and told him many were praying for him as he operated on Dave. He was silent for a moment; then, without acknowledging what I'd shared, he told me to follow him to ICU.

Beth, Thomas, and I had to wait outside Dave's door for quite a while until Dr. Constance reappeared, and when he did, he stated firmly, "You can take turns going in, only for a few minutes each, but I want you to be prepared. He's alive and conscious, yes, but he's been through a lot, and it will be a long road back. He'll need swallowing therapy, speech therapy, physical therapy, and more. We'll move him to the rehab building when he's able to leave ICU."

The doctor's words began to sink in, but all I could think was *Dave's alive! He's alive and conscious. That's all I care about. I'll be with him on the long road back. We all will. The Lord will be with him. I just want to see him.*

Those were my thoughts as I entered Dave's room, but then came another shock, followed by several more.

He was hooked up to tubes and wires and machines, and a nurse was hovering over him, checking him and all his "numbers." It was heart-stopping to see him like that.

I reached for his hand, amid all the wires, and he whispered, "Hi, sweetheart."

He didn't say more than that; he couldn't, but that was enough for me. He knew who I was and could say a few words. Thank the Lord. Thank the Lord.

Then, however, came the other shocks. The nurse explained that she needed to give Dave a test every fifteen minutes, around the clock, for several hours. I stood back and watched as she held up what looked like a large kindergarten book with four pictures on each page.

She first pointed to the picture of a hat and asked Dave what it was. He didn't know. Next, she pointed to a chair, and he didn't know what that was, either.

This continued with a few more pictures, and finally she said cheerily, "That's all right. You did fine. We'll try again in a little bit. Just relax now."

She motioned for me it was time to go, so I kissed my sweetheart and left with tears in my eyes.

Beth went in a few minutes later, and when she returned, also in tears, Thomas entered Dave's room. (Christopher was on his way across the desert from Scottsdale, and David on his way up from San Diego.) The three of us kept going in, when we could, and saw no change in Dave's ability to identify what was on the nurse's test chart. It was frightening, to say the least.

Then, at 7 p.m., we were told we couldn't go into the room again until 8:30, due to the nurses' shift changes. We'd need to leave for a while but could come back later. I decided it was a good time to go home to get some supplies because I was, of course, going to spend the night in Dave's room, that night and until I was convinced he was out of danger.

As I drove home, praying as I went, I thought how incredible it was that Dave was alive: an absolute miracle of God's grace. I thanked Jesus profusely and also wanted to thank

Dr. Constance again when I next saw him, and all the friends who were praying for Dave. I was so grateful to have a praying family and a supportive cadre of friends who were bringing my beloved husband to the throne of grace.

I gathered up what I needed from home and returned to the hospital, arriving there at 8:30, per the nurses' instructions. I expected to see a nurse, giving Dave the test they had been giving him every few minutes, the pictures of hats, and feathers, and chairs, and animals for him to identify (which, sadly, he had been unable to do).

But this time, when I walked hesitantly into his room, it was as though heaven had come down to Pasadena.

Dave was sitting up in bed and called out, "Hi, sweetheart! How are you? I'm doing great!"

A nurse was next to his bed, beaming from ear to ear, and before I could register my astonishment, she cried, "We've had a miracle! Your husband is back. It's absolutely amazing!"

I was so shocked, I could hardly catch my breath, as Dave broke in with, "I don't understand exactly what happened to me, but the doctor who just left told me I was paralyzed and almost dead. I had brain surgery but was still in bad shape after it, and then, suddenly, I recovered an hour ago. He said he has no explanation for my remarkable recovery. I told him that if my recovery was remarkable, then the Lord did it."

The nurse, who turned out to be a Christian, couldn't contain herself and interjected, "Praise the Lord. Praise the Lord!"

Minutes later, Christopher arrived from Arizona. (On the way to the hospital, he'd picked up his wife, Linda, and children, Lia and Kyle, who were already in Pasadena, visiting Linda's mother.) Christopher had begun driving across the desert from Scottsdale right after Beth called him, figuring it was actually faster to do that than trying to get to and from two airports and then to the hospital. When he walked into the room, to his amazement and utter relief, Dave welcomed him with, "Hi, son! They took some stuff out of my head this morning, and now I'm doing great. The good Lord brought me back."

I was holding one of Dave's hands, and Christopher grabbed the other one. We were astounded and thankful, so thankful that Jesus had intervened and saved Dave, and that his positive personality and down-to-earth self was also intact. Praise God, indeed.

The nurse took our hands, and she, Linda, Christopher, and I formed a prayer circle around the bed, praying for Dave and thanking Jesus for healing him and restoring him.

For the next two days, as nurses, family members, and friends came in and out of Dave's room in ICU, the theme was, This is amazing! Thank You, Lord.

Whenever someone would say, "You don't know what a lucky man you are," Dave would answer, "It wasn't luck; it was the Lord!" (When we saw our own family doctor and said, "It was the Lord," our doctor asserted, "You can say that again.")

The most impactful conservation, though, was with Dr. Constance, who had done the brain surgery. He came up to

Dave's room the night after he'd operated on him and was astounded at Dave's physical and mental recovery.

David, our oldest son, was still in the room as Dr. Constance pulled up a chair close to the bed; looking directly into Dave's eyes, he said, "Mr. Hanson, you are a very, very lucky man. Just hours ago, I was called in to do an emergency surgery just like the one I did on you yesterday. She was a woman exactly your age, with a blood clot in her brain exactly in the same spot yours was. I tried and tried for hours and couldn't dislodge the clot. I couldn't save her, and I'm devastated. Those with me in the operating room told me I needed to come up here to see you."

I had gasped when he said, "I couldn't save her," and my eyes filled with tears that began spilling down my face. David and Dave were silent.

Dr. Constance broke the silence and said again, "Mr. Hanson, you are a very, very lucky man."

Dave took the doctor's hand and, showing the emotion he'd been holding inside, repeated what he'd been telling everyone: "It wasn't luck. It was the Lord." But this time he added, "And the Lord used you to save me. Thank you, Dr. Constance. You helped to give me back my life. Thank you."

I echoed Dave's thanks, as did David; and, I hugged the doctor before he left and told him we would be praying for him. We also said we would be praying for the family of the woman who had been lost, and we did.

How sobering. Dr. Constance's visit had put it all in perspective. The Lord, for His reasons, which are so beyond our understanding, had saved my husband, had left him here on earth with us. "Awe" and "thankfulness" are words too light for what I felt ... and Dave felt ... and our family felt.

As Dave shared later, many times, "The good Lord left me here for a reason. He must still have things for me to do."

I'd answer, "Yes. You're still here to be my husband, the father to our children, and grandfather to our precious grandchildren, Lia, Beckett, Kyle, and Seth, who love you so much."

"Yes," he would reply. "That's all true, and there's probably something else too."

He was right. It was about that time our church asked him to be an elder, which is a big responsibility, timewise, workwise, and spiritually. Dave answered this call with an unquestioning affirmative. This was the "something else" the Lord still had for him to do, and he's done it with his usual gusto and joy.

EPILOGUE

Here's a postscript to Dave's stay in ICU:

Right after his surgery, Dr. Constance had said that Dave would need swallowing therapy, speech therapy, and physical therapy. Thus, after his miraculous recovery the night of his surgery, Dave was moved to the hospital's Rehabilitation Unit. There they tested him rigorously so they could begin the therapies needed. However, to their amazement (but not our amazement, at this point), the rehab specialists could find no impairment in any way. Dave was fine. His swallowing, speech, mental activity, and physical movements were perfect. Their tests confirmed that he didn't need therapy, and they recommended he be released from the hospital and sent home.

Therefore, on the fourth day (after a stroke, being paralyzed and unconscious, having brain surgery, and not knowing a hat from a chair), Dave was released and wheeled to the parking lot by a hospital attendant.

I walked ecstatically next to the wheelchair, calling our four children to tell them the great news, that Dad was going home. I was so engrossed in conversation with one of our children that I automatically jumped into the passenger seat and kept talking. Dave got in on the driver's side, and we took off. It wasn't until we were on the freeway, heading for home that I realized he was driving!

"The doctor probably wouldn't want you to be driving," I exclaimed loudly, as it finally dawned on me that he was behind the wheel.

"Why not? I'm fine," he answered, as he took the curves on the Pasadena Freeway like he always did, with his usual confidence.

As we rolled into our driveway, just days after the ambulance had sped off with Dave clinging to life, we thanked Jesus that Dave was a "walking miracle"; and, we still thank Him every day of our lives. "Thank You, Lord. Thank You, Lord."

"Then they cried to the LORD in their trouble, and he saved them from their distress. He sent out his word and healed them; he rescued them from the grave. Let them give thanks to the LORD for his unfailing love and his wonderful deeds for mankind." (Psalm 107:19–21 NIV)

"Fear not, for I am with you; be not dismayed, for I am your God. I will strengthen you, yes, I will help you, I will uphold you with My righteous right hand." (Isaiah 41:10 NKJV)

"Jesus went through all the towns and villages, teaching in their synagogues, proclaiming the good news of the kingdom and healing every disease and sickness." (Matthew 9:35 NIV)

(Old Testament, King David is speaking.)

"He said: 'The LORD is my rock, my fortress and my deliverer; my God is my rock, in whom I take refuge ... The LORD lives! Praise be to my Rock! Exalted be God, the Rock, my Savior!'" (2 Samuel 22:2, 3a, 47 NIV)

"Now to him [Jesus] who is able to do immeasurably more than all we ask or imagine, according to his power that is at work within us." (Ephesians 3:20 NIV)

A Prayer of Thankfulness for All of Us to Pray

Dear Jesus,

Thank You for all You've done for me and continue to do for me every day. Please keep me close to yourself, on Your path. I believe in You and love You. Thank You that You love me more than I can possible understand. Amen.

AN AFTERWORD

This touching afterword is about Dave's parents:

While looking through an old album containing pictures of Dave's parents' years in Alaska, I found this beautiful and touching narrative, written by them, about being far from home, in Alaska, on Christmas. When they speak of "the missionaries," they are speaking of themselves, and the two little "towheads" tucked into bed on Christmas Eve are Dave and his older brother, Paul.

"Christmas in the Arctic"

by

Alyce and Ralph Hanson

The Arctic sun rises at 10:30 p.m. and sets again at 1:30 a.m. However, the long Arctic night is at times as bright as day, with a full moon that seems to hang almost within your reach and bright stars that illuminate a deep blue sky with a million lights. Snow lies thick underfoot, and its chaste, white blanket lies glistening under the moon's bright rays, except where the feet of the Eskimos have tramped paths between the cabins. Spruce trees surrounding the village are also bedecked with snow, as though nature had caught the spirit of Christmas and was making all things beautiful for Christ's birthday.

It is very cold. The smoke from the chimneys of forty cabins on the hillside rises straight into the frosty air until far overhead. It blends into a great cloud overhanging the village.

The moon, so intimately near, the stars seeming to hover just above the cabins, the distant mountains and wooded slopes standing out so clearly in the bright light, give one the feeling of standing in the midst of a great infinity of space, and the thought of these infinite spaces impresses a great quietness on one's inner consciousness. But the spell is broken as an Eskimo sled dog at one end of the village lifts his shaggy head to the stars and gives voice to a weird, long drawn wail, which is as a signal to his kin to join in a mighty chorus, which surges through the village and culminates in a mighty crescendo of weird discordant sound.

You tremble a bit and perhaps shudder, but somehow that wild chorus expresses or gives voice to the deep emotions welling up within your own being, emotions which the Arctic night has inspired. As the howl of the dogs subsides, a cabin door opens, and a shaft of light stabs the night from a bright lamp within, and then the door slams shut again.

Suddenly, there is a cry: "Dog team! Dog team!" and there is heard the tinkle of bells, the crunch of sled runners in the dry snow, and the scurrying of padded feet as a dog team and sled glides swiftly into the village.

Every dog in the village instantly comes to life, and once again the mighty, weird chorus echoes and re-echoes as they greet their newly arrived brothers.

At last, the peculiar sounds of the Arctic night subside again, and now there floats out upon the still air the soft sweet strains of a hymn, coming from one of the cabins. A violin plaintively takes up the refrain of "Silent Night, Holy Night," and guitar chords join the melody so intimately associated with Christ's birthday.

A feeling of unspeakable sadness, loneliness, and longing for friends and loved ones so far away fills your breast. Time is forgotten, space is as nothing, life, and history too, crowd in upon one, all in a brief moment. This could almost be the night when angels heralded the coming of the Christ child to Bethlehem's manger, when glistening angelic hosts lit the sky with blazing grandeur.

Suddenly, a shaft of blazing light reaches its glistening hand out of the northern sky and pierces the atmosphere. As though it were a carefully planned attack, these mysterious beams of light from another world leap from the horizon and occupy our sky. Alternating shafts of red, green, and blue light surge across the sky in quavering streaks, from one end of the heavens to the other, now advancing, now retreating, like great armies locked in a death struggle, until the whole sky is ablaze with the supernatural light of the aurora borealis.

There is a loud shout, and soon cabin doors open and stalwart, brown-skinned Eskimos stand gazing up at this unearthly display with mingled feelings. Voices are hushed, the strains of violin and guitar die away into silence, and these hardy children of nature gaze upon this strange phenomenon with awe and fear. Again the frozen silence is cleft by the solemn wail of the sled dogs, troubled by the fearful display above, and again the mighty chorus echoes and re-echoes and then fades into the surrounding stillness.

The weird light warriors of another world retreat and leave the deep blue battlefield of the sky to the friendly light of the stars and moon. The Eskimos retreat to the warmth of their cabins, the violins and guitars resume their music, and the old men sit down and tell stories.

It is Christmas Eve. Eager-faced boys and girls within the warm cabins reflect the excitement and mystery of the occasion, speculating on what they will receive for Christmas. Parents within the confines of their small, one-room cabins try clumsily to conceal the contours of bulging packages underneath the bed or high on a shelf. Upon entering a cabin, we find a large group of the older people gathered, and they are singing a familiar melody, but the words are unintelligible to us. It is "All Hail to Thee, Oh Blessed Morn," but the words have been translated into Eskimo, and they sing that version to the original melody. They are practicing for the early-morning Julotta service and the Christmas church program that will be held the next day. In another cabin, we find a large group of Eskimo young people, and they are singing in harmonious strains as they practice familiar Christmas carols and choir anthems in the English language.

The church is beautifully decorated with two large, shapely trees, trimmed in tinsel and ornaments, standing on either side of the altar. Overhead are three illuminated stars. Slim white tapers and evergreen wreaths adorn the windows, and the pungent, delicious odor of spruce needles fills the air. The decorating committee takes one last look, an appraising glance at the result of their efforts, and with everything in readiness, leaves the room.

In the mission home, the missionary puts the finishing touches on his sermon and program for the early-morning service. His wife has already tucked bright-faced, anticipating little towheads into bed and is now busy in the kitchen, marshaling her stores of dainties and good food in readiness for the morrow. A beautiful tree stands in the corner of the living room, and piled beneath are many gifts, the kind remembrances from faithful friends and loved ones far away in the homeland. A warm fire roars in the radiating heater, and the room is illuminated by a gasoline lamp.

When all is in readiness, the missionaries retire, for four o'clock comes only too soon. They do not set the alarm, for they know that they will be awakened by a far sweeter sound than the harsh clanging of an alarm. They retire in silence, their hearts and minds wistfully occupied with thoughts of home and loved ones so far away.

Sleep comes quickly, and in their dreams, they resume the thread of thought and rejoice within the circle of friends and loved ones, as though they are actually together. But the dreams are jarred and torn between the vision of the subconscious and the reality of the impression borne upon the outward senses. The latter predominates, and coming to consciousness, they hear the crunching of footsteps in the snow outside their bedroom window. The dim rays of a lantern held high on a pole penetrate the window, and beautiful voices blend in rich harmony as they sing the beloved Christmas carols.

Their lonely hearts, mercifully drained of loneliness by sleep, are once again simply overwhelmed and flooded with loneliness and longing for loved ones and friends so far away. They listen quietly until the last sweet strains die away on the frosty air, and then they are jarred from their reverie by the shout, "Merry Christmas," from the voices of twenty or thirty carolers outside.

They dash out of bed, pull on their robes, rush to the kitchen, and seize large trays, already prepared and loaded with good things to eat; they go to the door to treat the carolers, who, having received the offerings, continue on through the village, pausing at each cabin to sing.

A warm fire is built in the church. The illuminated stars and candles are lit, and at 5:30, the deep and beautiful tones of church bells float out upon the frozen air. Soon, the church is filled, and the service begins. The hearts of the Christian Eskimos blend with their missionaries in pledging homage to and adoration of the Christ who came to Bethlehem's manger.

Among the many weird and mysterious sounds of the Arctic is heard the triumphant tidings that Christ is born. Having made their hearts a manger for the Christ child, having the glorious assurance of his abiding presence, their hearts are lonely no longer, and they rejoice with the Eskimo people and are glad upon the birthday of our Savior and Lord, who said, "Lo, I am with you always, even to the ends of the earth."

Printed in the United States
By Bookmasters